Over My Head

Over My Head

*The Power of Ancestral Music
to Future the Black Church*

LISA M. ALLEN

CASCADE *Books* • Eugene, Oregon

OVER MY HEAD
The Power of Ancestral Music to Future the Black Church

Copyright © 2025 Lisa M. Allen. All rights reserved. Except for brief quotations in critical publications or reviews, no part of this book may be reproduced in any manner without prior written permission from the publisher. Write: Permissions, Wipf and Stock Publishers, 199 W. 8th Ave., Suite 3, Eugene, OR 97401.

Cascade Books
An Imprint of Wipf and Stock Publishers
199 W. 8th Ave., Suite 3
Eugene, OR 97401

www.wipfandstock.com

PAPERBACK ISBN: 978-1-6667-8484-8
HARDCOVER ISBN: 978-1-6667-8485-5
EBOOK ISBN: 978-1-6667-8486-2

Cataloguing-in-Publication data:

Names: Allen-McLaurin, Lisa, author.

Title: Over my head : the power of ancestral music to future the black church / Lisa M. Allen.

Description: Eugene, OR : Cascade Books, 2025 | Includes bibliographical references and index.

Identifiers: ISBN 978-1-6667-8484-8 (paperback) | ISBN 978-1-6667-8485-5 (hardcover) | ISBN 978-1-6667-8486-2 (ebook)

Subjects: LCSH: Church music—United States. | African Americans—Music—History and criticism. | African American public worship

Classification: MT88 .A74 2025 (paperback) | MT88 (ebook)

06/20/25

In memoriam
Reverend Dr. Cecelia Williams Bryant
Bishop Anne Henning Byfield
Reverend Dr. Gay L. Byron
Reverend Dr. Barbara Ann Holmes
Reverend Dr. Love Henry Whelchel

For my ancestors, known and unknown

Contents

Acknowledgments   ix

Introduction   xi

1. African Traditional Religions: The Anchor for Music in African/African American Worship and Liturgy   1
2. Music and Worship Traditions of the Coptic and Ethiopian Orthodox Churches   15
3. The Significance of Spirituals to *AfricansinAmerica*   29
4. Hymnody in Black   41
5. The Emergence and Evolution of Gospel Music   54
6. Preserving the Gift of African-Descended Sacred Music in Contemporary Worship   67
7. Afrofuturist and Ancestral Worship Connections   83
8. Worship and Music Through an Afrofuturist Lens   103

Epilogue   131

Bibliography   135

Index   141

Acknowledgments

I WANT TO BEGIN by thanking the Sixth Episcopal District of the Christian Methodist Episcopal Church for encouraging me to develop my 2022 Winter Gathering presentation, entitled "The Importance of a Varied Music Program," into a book. I did not want to write a book only focused on musical genres, however, so I spent another several months considering what approach I would use to engage my love for Black sacred music genres. Enter Afrofuturism, a concept I became intrigued by following the publication of *The Dreamer and the Dream: Afrofuturism and Black Religious Thought* (2021), brilliantly written by my friend and colleague, Dr. Roger A. Sneed. He and the Rev. Amber Lowe Woodfork, a former student of mine and current PhD candidate at Indiana University, were invaluable conversation partners, outlining Afrofuturism's ideological framework and walking with me through possible practical applications and implications for the Black church. I would also like to thank the Phillips School of Theology and President-Dean Paul Brown for inviting me to present on Afrofuturism and worship at the 2024 Pastors' Conference, giving me the opportunity to share my research and receive significant feedback. The responses to my presentation ensured that I was, indeed, on to something that could benefit the church.

A special word of thanks to John Witvliet and Noel Snyder at the Calvin Institute of Christian Worship, as well as Matthew Wimer, Michael Thomson, and George Callihan at Wipf and Stock

Acknowledgments

Publishers/Cascade Books, for their encouragement and support through this process.

Last, as always, I want to thank my family, especially my husband, Thomas, our children and grandchildren, our extended family and friends, my MTSO community, especially Dean Valerie Bridgeman, and my ancestors, who continually show up and surround me with love and light as I co-create with the Divine to help build a future of beloved community.

Introduction

Oh, they tell me of a home, far beyond the skies.
Oh, they tell me of a home so far away.

—J. K. Alwood[1]

I BEGIN THIS BOOK with three confessions:

First, I have never been a sci-fi buff. While I can appreciate the groundbreaking work of Gene Roddenberry, George Lucas, and Stan Lee in creating alternate universes, I never gravitated toward the technological worlds of Star Trek, Star Wars, or superhero comic books. Whether the landscapes were too bleak, the jargon too technical, or the characters too weird looking, sci-fi as a genre did not attract me as a child. The only program I watched with any regularity that could be considered futuristic was *The Jetsons*. As an animated comedy, it was less threatening than other animated space stories and did not share the barren, desolate look of non-animated sci-fi shows. I found the modern mechanical and computer-generated conveniences interesting and imaginative, even though I considered the show unrealistic (how wrong I was!). As an adult, the only superheroes whose stories I've followed (mostly in movies) are the late Christopher Reeve's Superman, Wonder Woman, the Amazing Spider-Man, and the Black Panther. I was drawn to these characters because of their

---

1. Alwood, "Unclouded Day."

birth narratives, backstories, and how they were called to save their homelands and/or planet Earth. There was always a thread in their stories that resonated with me, with which I identified, and that kept me connected to and interested in their outcomes.

While not a sci-fi buff, I can, however, attest to being amazed at technological advancements that appear in many television shows and films, however imaginary or futuristic they may seem. Modes of travel, communication, medical techniques, and computer-assisted living make the world of the future seem quite attractive. I also appreciate how, in some media presentations, there is represented often a diversity of creation, whether human, plant, animal, android, or a combination thereof. Unfortunately, that diversity has not always included African or African-descended peoples or other persons of color in any great number. Further, I have noted how, despite all the technological progress future world inhabitants seem to have made, they are still beset by the same societal problems and issues impacting the twenty-first-century world. Greed, misuse of power, racism, sexism, heteronormativity, injustice, and oppression still run rampant in future worlds, despite all that has been done to create technological utopias.

Second confession: I have always been a music buff. I began playing piano at age three and taking piano lessons soon thereafter. As part of my weekly instruction, my piano teacher required me to complete music theory and history assignments. In each piano book were small biographies of the composers whose music I was learning, and often, there would be fascinating stories regarding their lives. As a dual piano and music education major in college, I continued to study the histories of composers, performers, and musical periods. I enjoyed making connections between music and world history, and often, these connections helped me remember dates and events that, otherwise, might have been difficult to memorize. Though twentieth-century classical music was not my favorite period, I did and still do enjoy reading the histories of and listening to contemporary R&B, blues, jazz, gospel, pop, funk, and yes, even disco music. It amazes me to hear the progression of twentieth- and twenty-first-century music, particularly from a

Introduction

technological viewpoint. The ways that computer technology has changed dramatically the production of music is astounding. The ability to imitate and manipulate voices and instruments, not to mention create all manner of sounds with mixing boards and synthesizers is both incredible and deceptive. It is quite common now to hear a recording artist live in concert and note how different they sound in person than on a recording.

While it may be disheartening to discover a favorite artist is not as talented as previously believed, the progress made in music through technology is not all negative. The ability to produce new sounds, tonalities, instrumental and vocal timbres provides listeners with imaginative, inspired works that propel us beyond the mundane or expected. Technological innovations in popular music from artists, producers, and engineers including Quincy Jones, Stevie Wonder, Les Paul, Maurice White of Earth, Wind, and Fire, Roger Troutman of Zapp, Jimmy Jam and Terry Lewis, Prince, Phil Collins, Peter Gabriel, Herbie Hancock, Teddy Riley, and Missy Elliott have expanded exponentially the work begun by computer music pioneers like Pierre Schaeffer, Raymond Scott, Morton Subotnik, John Cage, Philip Glass, and Sun Ra, one of the architects of Afrofuturism.

Third confession: I have always loved the church, particularly the Black church. My parents were both devout Christians and they believed in attending church regularly. Further, they believed in children attending church and fully participating in all activities designed for them. I sang in the children's choir, attended Sunday school and Baptist Training Union, and was a member of the church's Girl Scout troop. I was not alone; there were dozens of children who attended our church every Sunday and were involved in as many activities as I was. Yes, our parents made us attend; however, most of us continued to attend even after we became adults because being there had made a difference in our lives. The church nurtured us, trained us, taught us, gave us a place to shine, to belong, and to believe. The first place many of us ever publicly recited a speech, sang a solo, played an instrument, led a discussion, or conducted a meeting was at a church. We didn't just

Introduction

grow up in the church; the church grew up in us, and we became adults who understood the importance of community, the necessity of reading and study, the responsibility of leadership, and how spiritual formation functions as lifelong learning.

The church was, in part, responsible for my development as a musician, certainly as a church musician. I began as a child, playing for Sunday school, and then, as a youth, accompanying and singing in the youth choir and accompanying the senior choir. I continued playing through college and began to direct choirs under the tutelage of our directress, who had also been one of my first piano teachers. Serving in these capacities for decades steeped me in all genres of sacred music and allowed me multiple on-the-job training opportunities. I was able to learn, grow, make mistakes, and develop my musical and leadership gifts in an atmosphere of love and care.

In addition to my musical training, the church was one of the places I learned about what it meant to be Black. Every week, I heard stories and lessons about how the biblical text applied to the lives of African Americans, how God created and sustained us as a people, how the Holy Spirit empowered our ancestors to survive and thrive, and how Jesus walked with us, talked with us, and called us his own. There was no shame, no sin, no fault in being Black; in fact, it was something to be proud of and carried with it the responsibility of "lifting as we climbed." Our church, like many Black churches in the '60s and '70s, did not shy away from political involvement. We had several persons in our church and in our immediate community who served as elected officials, including our pastor, Dr. Horace L. Buckley Sr., and my uncle, Douglas L. Anderson Sr., both of whom served in the Mississippi state legislature. As a faith community, we knew the importance of voting in every election, of holding our elected officials accountable, of making sure school boards represented the best interests of our community's children, and of supporting the passage of legislation to ensure that historically Black colleges and universities of Mississippi received equitable funding each year.

Introduction

The music in our church reflected Black pride. We sang spirituals, lined hymns, and gospels with equal fervor and excitement. Our choral directors made sure we learned the histories of the songs we sang and their composers as well as the notes on the music staff. And we sang this music all year, not just in February for Black History Month. While our choirs sang anthems and classical works, including cantatas for Christmas and Easter, we did not prize this music over that of our ancestors. We valued each genre for its unique sound and contribution to the musical continuum. And we understood that singing the music of our ancestors not only served as fitting tribute to their imaginative artistry; it also signaled to us that, like our ancestors, we could sing the Lord's song in a strange land and use it to usher ourselves into our individual and collective futures.

Why did I begin with these confessions? Because this book is about the power of ancestral music, the Black church, and futuristic landscapes, and I wanted to be clear about how I've felt about each of those entities. I'm biased and want to acknowledge that bias before we go any further. Even though the Black church has struggled (and still struggles) with patriarchy, homophobia, and heteronormativity, I will not disavow her legacy nor the power of her ancestral music. I have spoken and fought against these oppressive issues and will continue to speak truth to power while loving and serving God's people to whom I feel called. Though I am not a lover of science fiction, I am committed to the stance that African and African-descended peoples are present in the future. That is why I am intrigued by the concept of Afrofuturism.

I became acquainted with Afrofuturism through the works of Roger Sneed and Ytasha Womack. Sneed's *The Dreamer and the Dream: Afrofuturism and Black Religious Thought* and Womack's *Afrofuturism: The World of Black Sci-Fi and Fantasy Culture* introduced me to Afrofuturism as a theoretical framework. After reading these, I realized I knew something of Afrofuturism as an ideological concept within speculative fiction from reading Octavia Butler's works, though I had not heard the term before. Womack quotes Alexander Weheliye, "The most important thing about

INTRODUCTION

Afrofuturism is to know that there have always been alternatives in what has been given in the present. I am not making light of the history of enslavement and medical experimentation, but black people have always developed alternate ways of existing outside of these oppressions."[2] Sneed states that Afrofuturism "is "a field of experimentation in which the Afrofuturist can engage music, art, or any other form of cultural production in order to center and reimagine Black lives and experiences."[3] As I read these works, it occurred to me that Afrofuturism, both as a concept and a framework have always been present in the ancestral music of *AfricansinAmerica*.[4] I found further evidence for my claim in Reynaldo Anderson's essay "Cultural Studies or Critical Afrofuturism: A Case Study in Visual Rhetoric, Sequential Art, and Postapocalyptic Black Identity." Anderson notes various rhetorical strategies which enslaved Africans employed as forms of resistance during the transatlantic slave trade, including signifying, call-and-response, narrative sequencing, and visual rhetoric, all of which are characteristics of African and Black ancestral sacred music.[5] Moreover, three of the fundamental qualities of Afrofuturism—imagination, hope, and the expectation for transformative change (what Womack calls the "through line that undergirds most Afrofuturistic art, literature, music, and criticism")[6]—are also threads that run through all Black ancestral sacred music and give it power.

In this text, I attempt to connect these threads of ancestral power of sacred music of Africans on North American shores with the spiritual power present in Afrofuturism and proffer how spiritual technologies present in the music of our ancestors

2. Womack, *Afrofuturism*, 39–40.

3. Sneed, *Dreamer and the Dream*, 23.

4. *AfricansinAmerica* is my term and is based on the work of Dr. Daniel P. "Omotosho" Black, professor of English and African American Studies at Clark Atlanta University. He asserts that the word "Black" is not truly representative of Africans and African-descended persons living in America. "Black" is a color; Africa is a continent. Therefore, those of African heritage living in America are *AfricansinAmerica*.

5. Anderson, "Critical Afrofuturism."

6. Womack, *Afrofuturism*, 43.

Introduction

can help future the Black church. Part 1 investigates the origins of African-descended Christian sacred music. Chapter 1 takes us back to Mother Africa, where we explore the uses of music in African societies, the various types of vocal and instrumental music and how they function in rites and rituals, and the use of music in worship. Of particular concern are the connections that can be made between African music used in worship and other religious ceremonies and the early development of Black sacred music on North American shores. Chapter 2 focuses on the origins and music of the two oldest Christian churches in history: the Coptic and Ethiopian Orthodox Churches. This chapter examines how characteristics of African music are present within the unique liturgical music of these churches and evince connections between this music and the music of enslaved Africans and their descendants during the antebellum period in North America. Further, chapter 2 initiates this book's ongoing conversation regarding how Black ancestral music can help *future* the contemporary church. Through investigating these churches in current contexts, we can see how faith communities are teaching both the retention of and adaptation of ancient ancestral liturgies and music.

Part 2 provides in-depth analyses of ancestral sacred music genres created and/or adapted by *AfricansinAmerica*, including spirituals, hymnody (including lined/metered hymns), and gospel music. Chapter 3 explores the creation of spirituals as an original art form arising out of an immediate need to lament the daily horrors of enslavement. In this chapter we ponder Dr. Katie Geneva Cannon's consideration of spirituals as folklore, "the indispensable device that slaves . . . used to transmit a worldview fundamentally different from and opposed to that of slaveholders."[7] Further, we assess spirituals as theological and ethical statements of belief, and question what significance spirituals have for contemporary worshiping contexts. Chapter 4 focuses on the development of a communal canon of song, specifically hymnody, in Black churches, both before and following emancipation. Like the chapter on spirituals, we note the presence of African musical characteristics

---

7. Cannon, *Katie's Canon*, 35.

INTRODUCTION

in Black hymnody, especially lined/metered hymns, which were traditional English hymns adapted to reflect African musical qualities. We also explore the development of traditional hymnody from English colonies through the Great Awakenings of the eighteenth and nineteenth centuries and consider what meaning hymnody holds for Black worshiping congregations in the twenty-first century. Chapter 5 details the emergence and evolution of gospel music as a vehicle for musical and lyrical experimentation, particularly in Northern urban metropolitan cities beginning with the Great Migration of the 1940s and '50s. Again, we investigate ancestral music connections and discuss their presence and evolution in contemporary gospel music of the twenty-first century, as well as the perceived significance of this genre to current worshiping congregations.

The final section of the book, part 3, launches the book into Afrofuturist mode, beginning in chapter 6 with how to preserve ancestral musical and spiritual legacies in each of these genres. We explore how, through research, teaching, and performances, churches can keep these genres an integral part of worship through the liturgical and calendar year. Chapter 7 provides detailed explanations and analyses of Afrofuturism as a concept and theoretical framework for *futuring* Black Christian faith communities. The chapter takes a close look at the decades-long decline in church worship attendance and the lenses through which people determine whether worship is meaningful for them. It describes how Afrofuturism provides both a *Sankofan* connection to the past and contains spiritual technologies of imagination, improvisation, and adaptability that help African and African-descended Christian communities engage the power to "vision" themselves into the future. The chapter concludes with a discussion on why an Afrofuturist hermeneutic is essential to Black Christian worship. Chapter 8 explores the use of this hermeneutic in planning and participating in worship. The first part of the chapter posits developing more liberative worship experiences through centering African and African-descended cosmologies, theologies, and hermeneutics, developing and implementing liturgies that affirm

Introduction

and center Black peoples and our experiences, and employing elements of worship that affirm and center Black ancestral practices and characteristics. The chapter culminates with a discussion of how Afrofuturism can help Black congregations discover, uncover, and recover the meaning and significance of our ancestral music lineages, through the practices of mythmaking, Conjure, and time-space exploration.

This book is by no means an exhaustive work on Black sacred music or Afrofuturism. Rather, it is an introductory treatise on how Afrofuturism might help the Black church thrive by remembering and reinvigorating herself through the music that helped birth and bring her and her people over. Though Afrofuturism is, by definition, a futuristic, and even abstract concept, at its core it contains ancient, ancestral techniques that can have very practical implications and impacts on the church's construction or reconstruction of her contemporary identity. Our music has always served as spiritual technologies, helping us "see" ourselves in the future. Afrofuturism provides a framework and vehicle for analyzing how this music has futured us and can continue to future us into eschatological realms and the world to come.

1

African Traditional Religions
The Anchor for Music in African/African American Worship and Liturgy

Siyahamba, ekukhanyeni kwenkos, Siyahamba, ekukhanyeni kwenkos.
We are marching in the light of God.
—Zulu Traditional Song

WHERE DO WE BEGIN the discussion about sacred music in the Black church? It must begin at its original source, Mother Africa. Whether the music that is being sung in worship today is traditional or contemporary gospel, contemporary Christian music (CCM), contemporary gospel-infused "praise and worship," spirituals, or hymnody, the origin of sacred music and the understanding of its meanings and uses in Black North American churches arose from our ancestral African lineages.

OVER MY HEAD

HOW MUSIC IS EMPLOYED IN AFRICAN SOCIETIES

Music making in Africa is categorized in three main sets of occasions: 1) work, 2) ritual, and 3) entertainment.[1] The nature of each of these is outlined below:

- Work—defined as manual labor and what is called "moral work." Music that accompanies this category includes work songs composed or generated by the activity itself, music to accompany domestic chores, and music for community activities. Music for moral work is designed to correct antisocial behavior through song. For example, rhymes created to tease adults who have violated a moral code.

- Ritual—defined as a set of processes conducted during a religious or solemn ceremony to mark a particular occasion or rite of passage. Music that accompanies rituals is specific to the occasion, including births, puberty and other age-related rites of passage ceremonies, marriages, deaths, funerals, festivals, and liturgical days, especially Sundays in Christian communities.

- Entertainment—including recreation and play. Music for these purposes may be performed by professional or nonprofessional musicians and may be as simple as children's game songs or as elaborate as royal music to entertain a monarch and guests.

It is important to note that in African countries, music is a communal enterprise, "a dynamic and driving force that animates the life of the entire community."[2] While some regions and towns may have professional musicians, including musical families or castes, there are others where anyone in the community may share in organic music production during daily activities by simply singing or providing body percussion. For many contexts, however, people

---

1. Agawu, *African Imagination*, 36.
2. Bebey, *African Music*, loc. 233 of 2648.

become musicians because of a social obligation to the community, which speaks to music's essentiality in African communities.

A specific category of professional musician that is important to mention is the *griot*, a West African term that designates a professional musician akin to a minstrel or troubadour. The *griot* is tasked with knowing the entire history of a people's traditions and producing appropriate music and stories for every occasion. Griots are paid to sing their benefactors' praises but enjoy universal admiration because of their virtuosity. Ironically, they are not personally appreciated or sought after *because* they know a village's or person's history and secrets. However, the *griot* is deemed significant in African societies because they hold a community's history and traditions while producing new music for said communities.

The overarching understanding of music in African societies is unlike that of European and Anglo-descended societies. Often, the latter see music as a means to an end, either the production of artistic beauty and/or a vehicle for profit. Though many African musicians may play professionally, the concept of music itself is viewed intrinsically, rather than extrinsically. Historian Francis Bebey offers an expansive description:

> What is music? It is the total expression of life, shared by all the senses. . . . Music is a challenge to human destiny, a refusal to accept the transience of this life; and an attempt to transform the finality of death into another kind of living.[3]

THE DRUM AND RHYTHM

According to Leonard Barrett, "The drum is Africa."[4] Historian Mechal Sobel states,

> Africans recognized the drum beat as a form of symbolic language, and many believed their sound was given to man by God as the third word. The rhythm of the primal

---

3. Bebey, *African Music*, loc. 1395 of 2648.
4. Barrett, *Soul-Force*, 82–83.

smithy, hammering out consciousness, shook and reverberated in the earth, transforming being.[5]

The drum provides rhythms, specifically African rhythms, which are unique to and among African peoples. Drums are perceived as the most representative African instruments, encapsulating what is meant by African music, identifiable by ever-present percussive rhythms expressing her people's deepest sensibilities. Even though particular tribes may use differing types of drums, various materials indigenous to their land, and even particular beat patterns that may be heard only in their area, there are common religious and musical aspects of rhythm shared among African societies. Jon Michael Spencer asserts the importance of the drum to African culture, stating, "In many traditional African societies the drum is a sacred instrument possessing supernatural power that enables it to summon the gods into ritual communion with the people."[6] Even drums that were not perceived in this manner were still regarded as necessary for performance in ritual action.

Though there is not space here to examine every type of drum, we will list some that play significant roles in African rites and rituals.

Hour-Glass and Slit Drum

The hour-glass drum is played by regulating forearm pressure to reproduce notes which represent words being transmitted. In Yoruba and certain Bantu languages, this method is used to play spoken phrases and can imitate nuances of speech including onomatopoeias. The slit drum can produce only two or three notes, which are coded and consist of metaphorical phrases which can be applied to various events.

---

5. Sobel, *Trabelin' On*, 80.
6. Spencer, "Rhythms of Black Folks," 39.

Single-Headed Drum

Single-headed drums are also used to send messages but may be played as part of drum orchestras, ideally consisting of six drums played as a "family," with "father" and "mother" drums and "four children" represented by smaller drums.

Friction Drum and Water Drum

The friction drum, played by exerting pressure on the drumhead to modify tension and vary pitches, gives an impression of a talking or singing animal, and can represent entities that watch over villages. The water drum is a large calabash filled with water played with a mallet. The water levels are changed to regulate pitches and "speak."

These drums produce rhythm, also an omnipresent feature of African music. While some may define rhythm technically, as the arrangement of downbeats and upbeats, like music, rhythm is defined much more existentially in the African consciousness. Again, Bebey elucidates this concept:

> Rhythm is an invisible covering that envelops each note or melodic phrase that is destined to speak of the soul or to the soul; it is the reflection of the consistent present of music. It is the element that infuses music with a biological force that brings forth a psychological fruit. Rhythm is a support or catalyst and not a musical form in its own right.[7]

Spencer argues that African rhythm was "the essential African remnant—the acme of Africanism."[8] He references the *ring shout*, as well as secular dances such as the *itch*, the *wringin'* and *twistin'*, the *black bottom*, and the *camel walk* that demonstrated the presence of "African movement motifs" that could be traced back to specific countries on the continent. Spencer argues that African drumbeats survived the *Maafa*, the auction block, urbanization,

---

7. Bebey, *African Music*, loc. 1436 of 2648.
8. Spencer, "Rhythms of Black Folks," 39.

and industrialization, because they were creolized and corporealized, meaning they were mixed with creole Africanisms and concretized through body movement.[9]

INSTRUMENTAL MUSIC

In addition to drums, there are a multiplicity of other instruments used in African music. While we cannot discuss all varieties within this context, we will review instruments in the four remaining classifications (membranophones having already been discussed).

Chordophones (Stringed Instruments)

Like drums, stringed instruments "speak," expressing various messages through the musician's gift, talent, and genius. Some are used in the performance of rites and rituals, while others are used to denote personal emotions or to share news, singing while being accompanied on a "talking" fiddle.

- The *konde* is a lute whose main purpose is to "speak" rather than to sing.
- The *wombi* is an eight-stringed harp which has been used in healing rituals.
- The *mvet* is a harp-zither used to accompany the *griot* in telling a story, usually tales of heroic deeds or legends of both mortals and immortals.
- The *bow-lute* accompanies magic incantations, especially of medicine men.

Aerophones (Wind and Air Instruments)

One significant characteristic of aerophones in African music is that there is no attempt made by the musician to modify their

---

9. Spencer, "Rhythms of Black Folks," 41.

timbre. Their sounds are left unaltered to be experienced purely as they are played.

- The *mirliton* is made from hollow bird bone, one end of which is stopped with a spider's web membrane. When it is played, the musician talks or sings with the mirliton in their mouth, and the membrane vibrates and "masks" the player's mouth. Mirlitons have many uses in African cultures, including adult rituals and as children's toys.
- Flutes come in three varieties—vertical, oblique, or transverse—and accompany rural herders who render sweet melodies to serenade their flocks. Flute duets are symbolic representations of marital unions and the fruit their unions produce.
- Trumpets and horns provide music for regal processions, funerals, battle entries and returns, and dance music for the royal court.
- The *alghaita* is a collapsible oboe which can produce a continuous sound if desired, in the manner of bagpipes, and has a distinct piercing sound capable of sending messages to those trained to decode them.

Idiophones (Instruments That Produce Sounds from Substances Not Stretched or Altered in Any Way)

- The *Sanza*, called "the little African piano," is known by many names and types, including thumb or hand piano. It is comprised of a sound box made of hollowed-out wood, with keys made of bamboo, bark, or metal, which are fixed to the soundboard and attached to the back of the bridge. The Sanza is not just used for recreation, but in many regions serves as a sacred instrument in rituals, including as a representation of ancestors. The *kalimba* is also a name for the thumb piano.

- The xylophone, an instrument with wooden bars or keys struck with mallets, can be found in many regions across the African continent. In some societies, xylophones were used historically in divination rites, where now they are mostly used to accompany dancing or in orchestras, blended with other xylophones or instruments such as the *Sanza*. Xylophones can also be used to represent speech, and in some music hold a "conversation" between the instrument and dancers.
- *Lithophones*, instruments limited to certain parts of sub-Saharan Africa, consist of a group of basalt stones which, when struck, produce sounds that can be incorporated into a piece of music. These instruments are used to mark agricultural seasons and feasts, and each feast rite has its own unique music that may not be used during any other season.

VOCAL MUSIC

While in the West the production of pitched sound, particularly in vocal music, is for the purpose of creating that which is most aesthetically pleasant, African music seeks to translate the mundane of everyday life into living sound. Vocal music plays an extremely significant role in this aim, first, because no one is hindered from participating in singing, and second, because everything that is expressible can be rendered with song. Rather than being concerned primarily with musical style or beauty, African vocal music "echoes the speech and thoughts of the community as faithfully as possible and without embellishment."[10]

What is most interesting in the African musical consciousness is that instrumental and vocal music do not compete with one another; rather, they complement each other, melodically, harmonically, and rhythmically. The prime objective of African music is to communicate language, and both voices and instruments

---

10. Bebey, *African Music*, loc. 1483 of 2648. Embellishment here refers to embellishment for artistic sake, i.e., vocal acrobatics such as arpeggios, glissandos, or melismata used to showcase the beauty of the voice.

accomplish this, in tandem with one another. Indeed, there is no distinction in the African musical consciousness between the human voice and musical instruments, which "speak" and express identical language and feelings when transforming thought into sound.

What were/are the meanings and uses of sacred music in African worship? While Africa is a vast continent, comprising many countries, peoples, and traditions, according to scholars, there are some common factors where worship and music are concerned. Most often, in African contexts, sacred music is employed in the extensive rites and rituals that accompany everyday life and in worship services of the various faith traditions of African peoples.

RITES AND RITUALS

Melva Costen asserts that "Africa is the anchor that holds music as the theological thread that runs through the fabric of African American existence," and "the musical anchor begins in rites and rituals of the community."[11] Religious rituals and worship experiences of *AfricansinAmerica*, no matter how extemporaneous or planned, followed certain African ritual and worship patterns. Theophus Smith defines ritual and its prominent place in African and African-descended cultures in North America as "a primal, and primary, mode of social interaction and performance."[12] The understanding of ritual as strategy in African culture is affirmed by Nya Taryor, who states, "Rituals also help the Africans to accept the claims of society in the new state. The individual can express his conflicts and tensions through ritual and resolve them. Africans use rituals of life's crises to provide them with needed emotional support."[13]

The legacy of African ritual as a practice was evinced in the ways that enslaved Africans and their descendants developed worship practices in the *invisible institution*. Homiletical theologian

---

11. Costen, *In Spirit and in Truth*, 3.
12. T. Smith, *Conjuring Culture*, 56–57.
13. Taryor, *Impact of the African Tradition*, 78.

Gennifer Brooks attests, "The hiddenness of the worship rituals of the captive people, exiled and enslaved far from mother Africa, was in direct response to the environment of slavery that had become their societal norm."[14] The use of ritual by *AfricansinAmerica* underscored the African cosmological worldview of sacred cosmos, which helped to identify and communicate "the reality of existential situations."[15] According to Costen, "Rites and rituals are forms of communication with the creator who established the cosmos, and a means of reactualizing the paradigmatic act of creation."[16]

How were music and dance used in African rites and rituals and how did those practices become part of the music and worship experiences of *AfricansinAmerica*? Dona Marimba Richards asserts, "A ritual is a happening; an event. It is a moment of eternity in which the right set of circumstances combines to create a transcendental experience."[17] *How* does this mean for the African? I use this phrase intentionally to clarify that ritual for African cultures cannot be expressed merely as a list of ceremonies or limited to tangible, empirical actions. Perceiving and engaging ritual are not a matter of "what," then, but "how." The concept of ritual is so pervasive in African cultures that the word "ritual" in John Mbiti's book, *African Religions and Philosophy*, is referred to on almost every page. Molefi and Kariamu Asante share this: "The ultimate expression of the African world view is the phenomenon of ritual. Only through ritual can death be understood as rebirth. It is through ritual that new life was given to the African spirit."[18]

The concept and habitation of ritual, by nature, are performative and dramatic. As Asante and Asante state,

> Ritual drama in African society is a multidimensional mechanism of cultural expression. It can be understood on metaphysical, religious, communal, and psychological

14. Brooks, "Africana Worship Ritual," 63.
15. Costen, "African Roots," 23.
16. Costen, "African Roots," 24.
17. Richards, *Let the Circle Be Unbroken*, 31.
18. Asante and Asante, *African Culture*, 218.

levels simultaneously. Ritual drama involves the repetition of a sacred act performed in a prescribed manner. It is religiously understood, therefore, as an imitation of divine beings or of our revered ancestors. Events are placed within the context of a harmonious order and so are sacralized. . . . African ritual drama is used to make transitions smooth, so that they will not disrupt the continuity of personal and communal life. . . . African ritual is a statement of continuity, unity, and community.[19]

The transmittal of African ritual and ritual practices on American soil, though unorganized and scattered, still managed to pervade and infuse Black antebellum worship. We have referred numerous times in this text to Africanisms and retentions present in these worship spaces, and their impact on the development of liturgical acts that arose and live, even today. Dona Richards offers insight into this presence: "Black life abounds with rituals through which we redefine ourselves as Black life by giving group expression to the African ethos."[20] *What* does this mean for *AfricansinAmerica*? Asante and Asante refer to the continuation of African ritual in the colonies noting,

> Spontaneous ritual drama was foreign to the Euro-American ethos and therefore could not have come from that source. We performed the "ring shout" in the "hush harbors," the night sings, and the "prayer meetin's." . . . We would form a circle, each touching those next to us so as to physically express our spiritual closeness. Through our participation in these rituals, we became one. We became again, a community.[21]

How did the perpetuation of ritual, even in abbreviated or syncretized form, help *AfricansinAmerica* navigate their existence and humanity in the New World? Carlyle Fielding Stewart contends that "through ritualization the unfamiliar become familiar; the unknown becomes known; that which alienates and dislocates

---

19. Asante and Asante, *African Culture*, 218.
20. Richards, *Let the Circle Be Unbroken*, 30.
21. Asante and Asante, *African Culture*, 217.

being and spiritual vitality becomes harmonized and ordered through the ceremonial invocation of the spirit and power of divine reality."[22] The ability to practice even a modicum of one's communal activities can precipitate *anamnesis*, and perhaps, transformation. Ritual practices, such as water baptism, conversion, spirit possession, funerals, and marriages, helped enslaved Africans and their descendants connect with the Divine and make meaning of their circumstances. Those members of the community who were designated as musicians carried the responsibilities of performing particular functions during rituals. Depending on what the religious and/or community leader hoped the ritual would accomplish, musicians performed their craft accordingly. Those who sang adapted their vocal timbres, inflections, pitches, scales, and harmonies to create resonant sounds to achieve the desired effects for a specific ritual. Instrumentalists manipulated their bodies and instruments to create the individual notes, collective rhythms, and accompaniments to create communal sounds that healed and uplifted the people. Engaging in these practices, both in the *invisible institution* and later in independent church congregations, aided *AfricansinAmerica* in bringing some semblance of self-ordering to their lives, and "codifying the structures of belief into stabilizing patterns of human existence."[23]

As enslaved *AfricansinAmerica* were introduced to and catechized into European/American Christianity, rituals they might have remembered and practiced in Africa were syncretized and synthesized into similar Christian practices. Whereas the practices and purposes of African rituals might have centered around the "High God," intermediaries, and/or ancestors, and might have been to achieve some tangible sign, message, or reward, the "ritual action in the Christian community of faith is founded on actions and words of Jesus, which are imbued with hope, fulfillment . . . and the essence of the gospel message."[24]

---

22. Stewart, *Black Spirituality*, 23.
23. Stewart, *Black Spirituality*, 25.
24. Costen, *African American Christian Worship*, 45.

African Traditional Religions

MUSIC IN WORSHIP

Just as there is music specifically composed and performed for certain communal rites and rituals, so too, there is music specifically composed and performed for worship services in African religious traditions. Scholar John Mbiti offers this description of African worship:

> God is often worshipped through songs, and African peoples are very fond of singing. Many of the religious gatherings and ceremonies are accompanied by singing which not only helps to pass on religious knowledge from one person or group to another, but helps create and strengthen corporate feeling and solidarity. . . . Music, singing and dancing reach deep into the innermost parts of African peoples, and many things come to the surface under musical inspiration which otherwise may not be readily revealed. These then are some of the ways African peoples worship God. They have no creeds to recite: their creeds are within them, in their blood and in their hearts. Their beliefs about God are expressed through concrete concepts, attitudes, and acts of worship.[25]

While there are an extensive number of traditions across African countries, there are common fundamental concepts that permeate worship practices, particularly the music that accompanies these practices. First is the concept of vocal music having the power to unify and transform communities, as singers and listeners. Second is the communal process of creating or re-creating songs, through composition, improvisation, adaptation, and modification, that speaks to the current situations and needs of those gathered. Third is that the music reflects African cosmological worldviews, including: 1) the belief in one supreme God (though in many Christian communities, this belief is inclusive of Trinitarian theology, to include the Son and the Holy Spirit); 2) an acknowledgment of communal solidarity, known as kinship; 3) respect for and acknowledgment of sacred cosmos; 4) the creation and presence of

---

25. Mbiti, *African Religions and Philosophy*, 65.

an African wisdom tradition; and 5) a holistic understanding of and desire for communal wellness and renewal.[26]

African Christianity exhibits these characteristics within its worshiping traditions, in both Orthodox and Independent Churches. However, it must be noted that the Christian church and its missionaries perpetrated irreparable harm on many indigenous worshiping traditions on the continent by denigrating, erasing, and even destroying many African traditional religious practices. Further, this mis-Evangelicalism found its way eventually into the indigenous Christian churches in Africa, including the Ethiopian church.[27] In the next chapter, we will examine the roots and development of music and liturgy of the two oldest Christian churches in the world, the Coptic Church and the Ethiopian Orthodox Church in an attempt to discover and recover the primal origins of the African Christian faith and their connections to the Black church.

---

26. Several of these cosmological worldviews are discussed in detail in ch. 8.
27. Nketia, *Music of Africa*, 13–19.

2

Music and Worship Traditions of the Coptic and Ethiopian Orthodox Churches

Now after they had left, an angel of the Lord appeared to Joseph in a dream and said, "Get up, take the child and his mother, and flee to Egypt."

MATTHEW 2:13

Oh, Mary, don't you weep, don't you mourn
Oh, Mary, don't you weep, don't you mourn
Pharaoh's army got drown-ded
Oh, Mary, don't you weep.

—TRADITIONAL SPIRITUAL

TWO MAJOR INFLUENCES AND connections in the development of African American Christian worship and music arise from the two oldest Christian churches in history, the Coptic Church and the Ethiopian Orthodox Church, both of which originated in Africa.

We will examine both traditions separately and then explore how they have influenced worship and music development in the African American church.

THE COPTIC CHURCH

Origins

The descriptor "Coptic" comes from the original name for Egypt, "Copt," derived from the term *kermit*, meaning "black." These descriptive terms refer to a geographical area in Africa located around the Nile River and the Rift Valley. The Gospel of Matthew records that, after the birth of Jesus, the holy family fled into Egypt to escape Herod's persecution of the innocents (Matt 2:13–23). According to church tradition, the holy family remained in Egypt for three years until Herod's death, and Coptic Christians claim as shrines many sites where they traversed and resided, on which now stand churches, monasteries, and convents dedicated to the Christian faith. Coptic historian Otto Meinardus asserts that "the first church built in Egypt was the Church of the Holy Virgin at the Monastery of the Holy Virgin in al-Qusiya, built immediately after Saint Mark the Evangelist's arrival in Egypt, sometime around A.D. 60."[1] Coptic Christians regard the apostle Mark as the founder of the Coptic Church and name him as the first patriarch of Alexandria. Meinardus recounts the story of how the apostle Mark the Evangelist converted Anianus, a shoe cobbler who pierced his hand while attempting to repair the evangelist's shoe. When he pierced his hand, Anianus cried out, "God is one," and the apostle Mark rejoiced, healed Anianus, and preached the gospel to him and his entire household, who believed and were baptized. After this, Mark ordained Anianus bishop, along with three priests and seven deacons, who greatly increased the numbers of Christian converts in the Coptic Church tradition.[2]

---

1. Meinardus, *Coptic Christianity*, 26.
2. Meinardus, *Coptic Christianity*, 29.

Music and Worship Traditions

Worship Traditions and Leadership

The Divine Liturgy is a public worship service in the Coptic Orthodox Church and consists of three parts: 1) the Offer of Oblation; 2) the Divine Liturgy of the Catechumens; and 3) the Divine Liturgy of the Faithful. The main subsections of almost all traditional liturgies, including Coptic ones, are: 1) Prayer of Thanksgiving, 2) Prayer of Consecration, 3) Prayer of Fraction, and 4) Prayer of Communion.[3] Three liturgies have been established in the Coptic church. 1) The Liturgy of Saint Basil is celebrated throughout the year except for the four major feasts of nativity, Epiphany, resurrection, and Pentecost; also, it is used daily in the monasteries whether there is a fast day or not. 2) The Liturgy of Saint Gregory is used today in the celebration of the four major feasts mentioned above; its music is somewhat more ornate than that of the Liturgy of Saint Basil and has been characterized as the most beautiful because of its high emotion. 3) The Liturgy of Saint Cyril, also known as the Liturgy of Saint Mark, is the most Egyptian of the three. Versions of St. Mark's Divine Liturgy exist in Geʿez, the ancient language of Ethiopia, which is the official and liturgical language of the Coptic Church of Ethiopia. Many scholars believe that most contemporary Coptic liturgies are derived from St. Mark's Divine Liturgy.

The celebration of the liturgy is preceded by two special services unique to the Coptic Church, of which one is observed in the morning just before the liturgy and the other the previous evening. They are known as the Morning (or Evening) Offering of Incense. In contemporary practice, the Morning Offering of Incense is often incorporated into the liturgy itself. Like the liturgy, these two services are cantillated. Scholar Melva Costen describes features of Coptic worship: 1) the Divine Liturgy is the central component; 2) worship spaces are dark, reminiscent of early churches; and 3) the liturgical pace is slow, and the congregation is invited to be emotionally and vocally involved in litany refrains.[4]

---

3. Coptic Orthodox Diocese, "Coptic Liturgy," 2.
4. Costen, *In Spirit and in Truth*, 20.

Over My Head

Music

Coptic liturgical music is monodic, vocal, and sung a cappella solely by men, except for some responses assigned to the whole congregation. One of the most obvious and common characteristics of Coptic music is the prolongation of a single vowel over many phrases of music that vary in length and complication. "This phenomenon may take two forms identified by scholars as *vocalise* (when the vowel is prolonged with a definite rhythmic pulse), and *melisma* (when the vowel is prolonged in a free, undefined rhythm). A melisma generally lasts from ten to twenty seconds, but some vocalises may continue for a full minute."[5] Small hand cymbals and the triangle are employed with specified pieces during certain services. The majority of texts in the Divine Liturgy are sung, with the exception of the Creed and Dismissal, creating a musical drama in three parts (mentioned previously): 1) the Preparation; 2) the Liturgy of the Word, also called the Liturgy of the Catechumens, which comprises the Prayer of Thanksgiving, the scriptural readings, various intercessions and responses, the recitation of the Creed, and the Prayer of Peace; and 3) the anaphora, the eucharistic ritual. The entire service may require some three hours of singing, and during Holy Week the special services may last six or seven hours.

The participants in the celebration of the liturgy and Offering of Incense are:

1. The officiant, that is, the priest and/or other high members of the clergy in attendance. The officiant recites prayers silently or sings them aloud. The construction of prayers follow psalmodic formulas, and can be simple melodies or contain extended melismata.

2. The deacon, who relays the officiant's requests, reads the lessons, and leads the set responses and singing of the congregational hymns. The deacon's cantillation involves more rhythmic melodic lines than the officiant's, with common use of vocalises and melismata. As soloists, both the officiant

---

5. Robertson et al., "Music, Coptic," 5.

and deacon have greater opportunities for improvisation and embellishment than the choir's selections.

3. The choir and/or congregation sing certain responses and portions of the hymns. In the early centuries, these sections were assigned to the entire congregation, but as the liturgy developed, they became so complicated that, eventually, a musically trained choir of deacons were assigned to sing them.[6]

THE ETHIOPIAN ORTHODOX CHURCH[7]

Origins

The *Kebra Nagast*, or the *Glory* or *Honor of Kings*, according to author John Binns, is the foundation narrative of Ethiopian Christianity, and makes a claim that "there is direct continuity between the Judaism of the Old Testament and the Christianity of modern Ethiopia."[8] The narrative asserts that the queen of Sheba visited King Solomon and later gave birth to their son, Menelek. When Menelek reached adulthood, he visited Solomon in Jerusalem and was crowned king of Ethiopia. As he prepared to return home, he dreamed that it was God's will for the ark of the covenant to go to Ethiopia with him. He took it back to Ethiopia, which, according to church tradition, accounts for the presence of Judaic practices and traditions in Ethiopian religion.

The arrival of Christianity in Ethiopia is primarily attributed to two Syrian boys, Frumentius and Aedesius, spared by "barbarians" after the ship they were on landed or wrecked on the Ethiopian coast, and taken to King Ezana's court at Aksum where they became his servants. Scholar Andrew Wilson-Dickson asserts both

---

6. Robertson et al., "Music, Coptic," 3–4.

7. "Administratively, the Ethiopian Church was part of the Coptic Orthodox Church from the first half of the 4th century until 1959, when it was granted autocephaly (full independence) by the Pope of the Coptic Orthodox Church." Association of Religion Data Archives, "Ethiopian Orthodox Church," para. 1.

8. Binns, *Orthodox Church of Ethiopia*, 46.

boys were Coptic Christians,[9] while Binns states it was Frumentius who sought out "Roman" Christian merchants for places to have prayer and went out "promoting the seed of Christianity in the country." Athanasius consecrated Frumentius as the first bishop of the Ethiopian Orthodox Church, "marking the beginning of the Christian Church in Ethiopia."[10]

Worship Traditions and Leadership

The Ethiopian Orthodox Church developed a unique liturgical language, Ge'ez, which is still used in religious services today. The liturgy is characterized by elaborate rituals, chants, and prayers known for their "rich poetic language and deep theological content."[11] The Divine Liturgy, also known as the Holy Qurbana, is celebrated on Sundays and holy days, and includes the Eucharist, prayers, hymns, and biblical readings, arranged intentionally to facilitate a profound spiritual experience with and in the presence of God. In addition to these services, there are special liturgical texts for baptisms, weddings, and funerals, as well as a comprehensive set of daily prayers, called the Daily Offices, designed to help keep the faithful connected to the Divine.[12]

The Divine Liturgy according to the Ethiopian rite is divided into two parts, 1) the introduction, called the *Ordo Communis*, and 2) the eucharistic part called *Anaphora*. The order of worship consists of the following:

> Part 1: *Ordo Communis*:
> The greeting of the priest to the faithful and their response
> Readings and hymns
> Gospel and homily
> Dismissal of the catechumens
> The kiss of peace

---

9. Wilson-Dickson, *Story of Christian Music*, 163.
10. Binns, *Orthodox Church of Ethiopia*, 72–73.
11. Oatman, *Ethiopian Orthodox*, 41.
12. Oatman, *Ethiopian Orthodox*, 41.

Music and Worship Traditions

Part 2: *Anaphora* (the Eucharist)

There are two types of services, indoor and outdoor. Indoor services are conducted in the holy of holies by a minimum of five persons, two priests and three deacons. Outdoor services are conducted by priests and *dabtaras* (musicians). The celebrants are required to abstain from food for at least twelve hours in advance. The normal duration of a service is about two hours, but it may be lengthened or shortened upon occasions.[13] All liturgical leaders, including priests, deacons, monks and *dabtaras*, are required to know the music of the liturgy. *Dabtaras*, scholars who must complete at least a decade-long course of study in *zema* (sacred music), *aquaquam* (sacred movement), and *qene* (poetry of the church), hold an essential ministry as "lay ecclesiastics/canons/choristers" and are required to preserve and pass on the church's artistic tradition.[14]

Music

According to church tradition, the sacred chant of the Ethiopian Orthodox Church was created by Yared, who came to Ethiopia in 457 CE (other narratives date him to the early sixth century). Yared was sent to study and, from listening to birds singing, learned a new style of chanting, "a high tune," rather than the previous singing style which "had been a soft whisper in the throat." His hymns follow the Semitic tradition of poetry, building up a series of images of ideas, referencing Scripture and teachings which combine to create "an evocative style of Christian teaching."[15] Jesuit priest Jerome Lobo offered these characteristics of the music of the Ethiopian liturgy:

> The instruments of Musick made use of in their rites of
> Worship are little Drums, which they hang about their

---

13. Sellassie and Mikael, "Worship in the Ethiopian Orthodox Church," s.vv. "2. The Times of Worship: Church Services."
14. Binns, *Orthodox Church of Ethiopia*, 271–72.
15. Binns, *Orthodox Church of Ethiopia*, 249–50.

Necks, and beat with both their Hands these are carried even by their Chief Men, and by the gravest of their Ecclesiasticks. They have sticks likewise with which they strike the Ground, accompanying the blow with a motion of their whole Bodies. They begin their Consort (that is, music-making) by Stamping their Feet on the Ground, and playing gently on their instruments, but when they have heated themselves by degrees, they leave off Drumming and fall to leaping, dancing and clapping their Hands, at the same time straining their Voices to the utmost pitch, till at length they have no Regard either to the Tune, or the Pauses, and seem rather a riotous, than a religious Assembly. For this manner of Worship they cite the Psalm of David, "O clap your Hands, all ye Nations."[16]

Music historians assert that the Ethiopian Orthodox Church's sacred music is central to and enhances her liturgy, using intricate melodies and harmonies that liturgical leadership has devoted a lifetime to learning and perfecting. Use of traditional musical instruments including the *begena* (a ten-stringed lyre), the *masenqo* (a single-stringed fiddle), and the *tsenatsil* (a type of sistrum) add distinct textures which blend with choral voices to produce a uniquely vibrant sound, connecting the contemporary worship space with ancient liturgical traditions.[17]

TIES TO THE MUSIC OF AFRICAN AMERICANS IN THE ANTEBELLUM PERIOD

How is the music of the Coptic and Ethiopian Orthodox Churches related to the sounds and consequent genres of music created/produced by African Americans during the antebellum period? Characteristics of early African American music include: 1) a cappella singing; 2) vocal ululations (howls, wails, groans, shouts); 3) call-and-response as a singing method; 4) extemporaneity and improvisation; 5) use of long, melodic lines and melismatic

---

16. Cited in Wilson-Dickson, *Story of Christian Music*, 162–63.
17. Oatman, *Ethiopian Orthodox*, 53.

embellishment; and 6) storytelling in song. From the accounts of musical styles in worship in both Coptic and Ethiopian Orthodox Churches, we can attest to the presence of all these characteristics. A cappella singing in worship was a given during the antebellum period as there were few, if any, keyboard instruments available and stringed accompaniment would have been considered secular entertainment. Moreover, African Americans worshiping in the br(hush) arbor would not have used instruments, even if they had been available, to keep the sound volume as low as possible.

The sacred chants used in both churches require liturgical leadership to be adept at leading with solo voice, while choirs and/or congregations respond, either with monodic chant or chordal harmonies. Soloists are allowed to sing extemporaneously, employing complex vocalises and extended melismatic lines. The testimony given by priest Jerome Lobo regarding the music of the Ethiopian liturgy, which begins with drums and body percussion and, as the Spirit descends, escalates into full-throated singing and shouting with dancing, resembles quite closely the depiction of an African American ring shout. Further, the use of body percussion and simple stringed instrumentation recalls the use of hand clapping, foot stamping, drums (or other percussive production), fiddles, and banjos of early African American praise house worship or recreational activities.

ANCESTRAL TIES AND AFROFUTURIST PROJECTIONS

What of these ancestral ties can help us project into the future? How do/can the music and worship traditions of ancient churches help the contemporary church future itself? To help answer this question, I want to employ two texts that have been extremely instructive in this effort. The first is a 2015 article about an American Coptic community where young people are being taught ancient liturgies. The second is Leonard McKinnis's text *The Black Coptic Church: Race and Imagination in a New Religion*. Author Teresita Lozano introduces her article, "'It's a Coptic Thing': Music, Liturgy, and Religious Identity in an American Coptic Community," with the following statement:

> At St. Mark Coptic Orthodox Church in Englewood, Colorado, the community utilizes its liturgical performance to express its spirituality and negotiate its Egyptian-Coptic identity. It sustains this identity by creating a cantillation school, in which the American-born youth, who are largely not fluent in Arabic or Coptic, are educated in the music and culture of the tradition. The adaptation of English to Coptic hymnody and the ability to participate in the celebration enable the youth to maintain and express a complex identity, rooted in their parents' Egyptian Coptic heritage and their own American experience.[18]

Throughout the article, Lozano describes the church, its liturgical worship, and the work of the priest, Father Yacob, who helps the young boys learn, participate, and lead ancient Coptic worship. She recounts Father Yacob's desire to "keep the rituality of the liturgy as it is performed in Egypt," by teaching the youth "what it means to be a Coptic Orthodox Christian in the United States."[19] To ensure these youth can learn and demonstrate liturgical actions, St. Mark's holds cantillation classes where a lead cantor teaches students of all ages and skill levels through the oral tradition, in ways identical to the traditional chant education done in Egypt. Younger children begin by learning basic chants and, as they mature, learn more difficult chants, all done through a process of repetition and weekly rehearsals. Further, those taking classes are expected to participate in Saturday Vespers, which allows for immediate application of what they have learned during the week, helping them build a "memory bank that will eventually allow them to appropriate different texts to specific melodies based on the feast and season . . . going beyond a one-dimensional aspect

---

18. Lozano, "It's a Coptic Thing," 37.
19. Lozano, "It's a Coptic Thing," 46.

of learning and focusing on attending the Divine Liturgy and appreciate what attending the Divine Liturgy signifies."[20]

What would it mean to replicate this model in African American churches today, to implement a music education system designed to teach children and youth the music of our ancestors and how it applies in worship settings? While there are churches that have children's and youth choirs, are they learning ancestral music (lined hymns, traditional hymnody, spirituals, gospels), or only children's songs, top-forty contemporary gospel, or popular CCM songs? Why is it important that they learn historic music and worship traditions? Father Yacob offers a response: "Liturgical participation and chanting are a way of not only expressing and performing spiritual heritage, but taking on the role of a servant to the congregation."[21] Lozano continues, "The young cantors are embodiments of transmission and preservation of their spiritual heritage, transporting the congregation back to the Coptic churches of Egypt and recreating a spiritual homeland within the physical and cultural boundaries of an American space . . . young cantors view participation in liturgical cantillation as worship, but also as cultural communication in the context of Coptic worship, and as community service."[22]

The Black Coptic Church explores the origins and development of a religious movement developed in the wake of the Great Migration which retained elements of Christianity. According to McKinnis:

> The Black Coptic Church combined elements of Black Protestant and Black Hebrew traditions with Ethiopianism, providing a divine racial identity and a royal Egyptian heritage for its African American followers—a heroic identity that was in stark contrast to the racial identity imposed by the white dominant culture. . . . Black Coptics embrace the idea that Black people are the

---

20. Lozano, "It's a Coptic Thing," 49.
21. Lozano, "It's a Coptic Thing," 50.
22. Lozano, "It's a Coptic Thing," 51.

"chosen people," and thereby embody a sense of divinity due to their relationship to God.[23]

Though the Black Coptic Church (BCC) does not have an ecclesial relationship with the Coptic Orthodox Church, the church's founder, Prophet Cicero Patterson, named it such as a way of helping Black people connect the ancient Egyptian Christian heritage with their own North American location. The BCC asserts that Black people are of Ethiopian descent, if not genetically, certainly ideologically, which provides Black people a sense of history that predates American slavery. Thus, Black people can perceive themselves outside the white gaze, without stereotypical tropes constructed by white supremacist notions of inferiority and subhumanity. The ability of African Americans to imagine ourselves in full personhood, with whole souls and bodies, would have been a novel (and dangerous) concept during the antebellum period (and even beyond), as most of what our ancestors heard and were taught in slaveholder churches was that they were nonhumans without souls, whose bodies belonged to those who claimed to own them. Though some would have countered these notions in br(h)ush arbor and praise house worship, many more internalized this identity and carried it with them, even into emancipation. The BCC's founder, Prophet Cicero, sought to dismantle what McKinnis calls "the existential absurdity, loss of identity, and religious isolationism" our ancestors encountered in white Christianity and some Black mainstream religions.[24] In Cicero's Spiritualist tradition, he was making a connection between religious identity and Black emancipation, in which "black life, black culture, and black religion flourished and were celebrated."[25]

If the Black church is to thrive, it matters that our children and youth are taught the liturgical traditions of our ancestors. Almost every Black church across every denominational strand and hue is lamenting the dearth of children and youth in worship. It

23. McKinnis, *Black Coptic Church*, 4–5.

24. McKinnis, *Black Coptic Church*, 48.

25. McKinnis, *Black Coptic Church*, 52, citing an interview with Queen Huldah.

Music and Worship Traditions

is the parents' or guardians' responsibility to bring them, but it is the church's responsibility to provide them a sense of meaning and continuity; places and spaces where they can learn what it means to be a part of that particular local congregation, and also what it means to be a part of a larger faith community, religiously and culturally. If children and youth are to learn our music histories, we first must find these histories important enough to teach and program into weekly services. We can't trot out spirituals, lined hymns, and traditional gospels once a year during February or church anniversary programs and expect young people to find them valuable enough to commit to learning them and being present on a regular basis to sing them. This music is part of our spiritual heritage, what links us with and helps us connect to the Divine, in ways that contemporary music often does not have the power to do.

Afrofuturist worship, worship that asserts and affirms that Black people are present in the future in holistic, thriving communities of faith, demands that we use a *Sankofan* lens to go back and fetch from the past what was essential, formative, and transformative in our ancestral music and worship. Thus, we are clear we have always been believers in the Divine, have always been creative, dynamic, intellectually astute people who have and continue to use spiritual technologies to experience, produce, and develop that which affirms our holistic existence and our connection with the Divine. Prophet Cicero's Black Coptic Church is one such example of Afrofuturist worship, as McKinnis notes, "It is a collapsing of time, namely the bridging of history, the future, and the present, as a performance of the Church's idea of freedom."[26] Further, the BCC's understanding of its women and men as royalty, as queens, princesses, kings, and princes, provides a cultural aesthetic of Black people as inherently worthy and able to project and create their own living futures, redeeming Black life from death-dealing modalities and anti-Black imaginaries.[27] Teaching our children and youth that they are descendants of African royalty whose

---

26. McKinnis, *Black Coptic Church*, 81.
27. McKinnis, *Black Coptic Church*, 81, 122.

music and liturgical traditions served as foundational to the development of the Black church *is* Afrofuturist because it is employing spiritual technologies embedded in sacred music and worship to link a sacred, ancestral past with an imaginative, divine future.

The following three chapters explore the sacred music of our ancestral past on North American shores, their origins and evolution, and the significance of spiritual technologies they contain which have nurtured, sustained, and moved *AfricansinAmerica* ever forward.

3

The Significance of Spirituals to *AfricansinAmerica*

> *Over my head, I hear music in the air*
> *There must be a God somewhere!*
> —TRADITIONAL SPIRITUAL

IN 1992, JAMES CONE authored *The Spirituals and the Blues*, a text that expanded his exploration of Black folklore in his earlier work, *God of the Oppressed*. In this book, Cone provides context for the historical development of and theological assertions inherent in these two genres of music. He presses his claim throughout the text that "the power of song in the struggle for Black survival—that is what the spirituals and blues are about."[1]

In 1995, Katie Geneva Cannon authored *Katie's Canon: Womanism and the Soul of the Black Community*, a semi-autobiographical collection of essays, exploring "Black Women's Literature as Sacred Texts."[2] In her text, she lays the foundation for

---

1. Cone, *Spirituals and the Blues*, 1.
2. The title of Dr. Cannon's presentation at Michigan State University in the fall of 1985, after which Dr. Bernice Johnson Reagon suggested Dr. Cannon

"womanist norms as emancipatory praxis."[3] In her essay "Surviving the Blight," Cannon discusses the cultural inheritance of Black folklore, including spirituals, which she describes as "the indispensable device that slaves . . . used to transmit a worldview fundamentally different from and opposed to that of slaveholders."[4]

Spirituals, also called Negro spirituals, are considered by many scholars and historians the first original American music.[5] Named "sorrow songs" by W. E. B. Du Bois, they were born out of the field hollers and plaintive cries of enslaved Africans and their descendants on American shores. Expressions of lament, grief, anger, hope, and even joy can be heard in the lyrics while the music and rhythms are primarily of African origin. As noted by Du Bois, Cone, and Cannon, spirituals were and are a significant part of African-descended folklore, part and parcel of rituals and traditions handed down for generations, which transmitted theological and ethical systems of belief, being, and becoming. Historian Albert Raboteau remarks, "The flexible structure of the Spirituals allowed the slaves to comment on the daily events of their lives, so that the community heard and shared the cares and burdens of the individual expressed through song."[6] Before the first *AfricansinAmerica* were allowed to enroll in a seminary, allowed to study by lamplight the mysteries of God, even before the first enslaved person risked death by learning to read, spirituals communicated to African-descended persons what it meant to be Black in America. Spirituals were theological affirmations; they affirmed who God was, to and for Black people in America. They were ethical assertions and admonishments of how to act as Black people in America, and conversely, how to face being acted upon by others.

---

take on the task of "opening up the canon." Noted in Cannon, *Katie's Canon*, 17.

3. Cannon, *Katie's Canon*, 17–18.

4. Cannon, *Katie's Canon*, 35.

5. See Cone, *Spirituals and the Blues*; Southern, *Music of Black Americans*; and Abbington, *Readings*, vol. 1.

6. Raboteau, *Canaan Land*, loc. 445 of 1424.

The Significance of Spirituals

Musically, spirituals bore an African identity, utilizing pentatonic and other African scales and modes melodically and harmonically, polyrhythms and syncopation, segmented and repeated melodic phrases, and spontaneous tonal combinations and cadences. The use of plaintive melodies with flatted third and seventh notes, call-and-response phrases, and extemporaneously improvised refrains and choruses are all retentions that crossed the Atlantic with our African ancestors. Other characteristics include the use of texts from daily life experiences, the world of nature, personal experiences, and the biblical text, the use of coded messages, symbols, and imagery, and recurring themes of hope for liberation. While spirituals originated in rural agrarian communities as an oral/aural tradition, with each singer or group performing the melodies, harmonies, and rhythms as they chose within a particular moment, as they became popularized,[7] they required codifying for publication. From the late 1800s, composers and scholars have transcribed and compiled collections of these works for publication and performance, including William Allen's *Slave Songs of the United States* (1867), J. B. T. Marsh's *The Story of the Jubilee Singers and Their Songs* (1881), Samuel Coleridge-Taylor's *Twenty-Four Negro Melodies, Transcribed for the Piano* (1905), Henry F. Krehbiel's *Afro-American Folk Songs* (1914), R. Nathaniel Dett's *Religious Folk Songs of the Negro as Sung at Hampton Institute* (1927), Miles Mark Fisher's *Negro Slave Songs in the United States* (1953), and James Weldon Johnson and John Rosamond Johnson's *American Negro Spirituals* (1977).

Spirituals as Folklore

Dr. Cannon describes folklore as "a strategy for coping with oppression,"[8] a method of using coded language to communicate messages that would have been dangerous to state openly. Through stories, children's rhymes, games, and music, *AfricansinAmerica*

---

7. Spirituals became popular performance pieces due in part to the international tours of the Fisk Jubilee Singers and subsequent performing groups.
8. Cannon, *Katie's Canon*, 33.

talked and sang about how the supposedly stronger, smarter character was constantly bested by the weaker, ignorant one. This was a way to launch a direct attack on their oppressors without suffering retaliation. Dr. Cannon continues, "Folklore was the essential medium by which the themes of freedom, resistance, and self-determination were evoked, preserved, and passed by word of mouth from generation to generation. . . . By objectifying their lives in folktales, Afro-American slaves were able to assert the dignity of their own persons and the invincibility of their cause."[9]

Spirituals are characterized as folklore because they were created as a coping mechanism for *AfricansinAmerica*. African chants and melodies that arrived on slavers' ships could not be silenced, even in the face of brutal treatment, and they rose on the lips of the washerwoman, the field hand, the cook, and the medicine wo(man) in daily life. They gave voice, in a socially acceptable way, to the captive, socially unacceptable emotions coursing throughout African and African-descended bodies. In them were present the themes of freedom, resistance, and self-determination, though they were often received as harmless by the oppressor. Spirituals such as "Oh Lord, How Come Me Here?" and "Sometimes I Feel Like a Motherless Child" bespoke the despair and anguish felt by those who could find no reasonable rationale for their plight. In these, the singer expresses genuine bewilderment and even abject resignation to the hopelessness of a situation over which there is no apparent escape. "All God's Chillun Got Shoes" was a veiled jab at slave owners who didn't provide sufficient clothing for those they enslaved, while also calling into question their heavenly reward ("Everybody talkin' 'bout heaven ain't goin' there"). Other spirituals using coded language to refer to freedom and possible attempts to escape to freedom include "Oh, Freedom," "Steal Away," "Follow the Drinking Gourd," and "Deep River." *AfricansinAmerica* learned and sang these songs as a way of dealing with the horrific and cruel treatment inflicted upon them by many who proclaimed themselves "Christian" but who certainly didn't behave in any way "God conscious" as Africans understood the concept.

9. Cannon, *Katie's Canon*, 34.

The Significance of Spirituals

Spirituals as Theological and Ethical Statements of Belief

In some sense, it has been a prevailing (and incorrect) assumption that Africans who were brought to America during the transatlantic slave trade had no concept of God. To the contrary, scholars John Mbiti and Melville Herskovitz, among others, argue that Africans lived under a cosmological worldview that included belief in a supreme deity.[10] In many African traditional religious belief systems, the supreme deity was assisted by lesser gods who mediated between the supreme deity and humans. As *AfricansinAmerica* were introduced (and some reintroduced) to the European/American version of the Judeo-Christian faith, they made parallels to the God/s of their ancestors, and spirituals reflected these parallel understandings about who God and Jesus were for them.

Dr. Cone asserts that, theologically, spirituals spoke of God primarily as Liberator. Songs such as "Didn't My Lord Deliver Daniel" and "Go Down, Moses" employed biblical language to remind the singer (and listener) that, just as God had delivered God's people in the Bible, God would deliver *AfricansinAmerica* also. Jesus was perceived as suffering servant, but with just as much power as God. He was the "Little Innocent Lamb," the "Lily of the Valley," but also the "King of Kings." Jesus, like God, was Liberator, divine, but also human, "Mary's Little Boy-Child." Enslaved Africans identified with Jesus because he was born poor, in a stable, but grew up with the power of God on and within him, and because of this power, Jesus was able to bring good news to the poor and lift them up out of their misery. Moreover, enslaved Africans were able to identify with Jesus because he was brutally mistreated and killed, though he had done nothing wrong. Paradoxically, this gave meaning to their struggle to live (and live purposefully) in the face of imminent suffering and death. Spirituals like "Give Me Jesus," "He Never Said a Mumblin' Word," "Listen to the Lambs," and "When I Die, I Want to Die Easy" give voice to the enslaved

---

10. See Mbiti, *African Religions and Philosophy*; and Herskovitz, *Myth of the Negro Past*.

African's understanding of what it meant to live and die, believing that one had lived as righteously as possible in the face of death.

AfricansinAmerica perceived theological and ethical concepts such as sin, evil, and judgment as directly related to their suffering. Sin was the result of broken relationship with God, characterized by the brokenness of humanity that allowed for their captivity and oppression. Evil was the embodiment of Satan's influence and power, characterized by the actions of their oppressors. To be sure, *AfricansinAmerica* understood that they could be sinners (those who refused to live according to God's commands regarding righteousness), but true evil was that which was perpetrated upon them by slave owners and those who worked for the slave owner. Evil was that which hampered the African's desire for and realization of liberation and justice, as well as the inhumane treatment experienced because of enslavement. Spirituals that addressed Africans' personal understanding of sin included "Sinner, Please Don't Let This Harvest Pass," "I Believe I'll Go Back Home," and "Standing in the Need of Prayer." Those that referenced Satan and the concept of evil include "Shut de Do," "Go 'Way, Satan, I Doan Mind You," and "Ezekiel Saw de Wheel." Judgment was the clear result of God's power against those who victimized the innocent and weak. The eschatological hope in the power of God as supreme deity, in Jesus' resurrection ("He got up with ALL power in His hands!"), and in the cosmological understanding of judgment as the "setting right" of all earthly things lived in the lyrics of spirituals such as "I'm So Glad Trouble Don't Last Always," "Soon One Morning," "Oh, Mary, Don't You Weep," and "My Good Lord's Done Been Here."

The Import and Implications of Spirituals for Twenty-First-Century AfricansinAmerica

When I serve as a church musician, I always present a varied program of music. I make sure choirs and congregations sing hymns, anthems, gospels, *and* spirituals. Very rarely do I receive any pushback or critique on hymns, anthems, or gospels, but invariably I

The Significance of Spirituals

receive at least a few negative comments about singing spirituals. I hear statements like, "We don't want to sing this 'slave' music," "This music is depressing," or "This music isn't relevant for Black people anymore." I counter by telling choirs, "This is the music of our history and heritage. If we stop singing it, we forget it, and soon, we will forget our history and heritage." But the statement about relevance always intrigues me. Are spirituals still relevant for *AfricansinAmerica* in the twenty-first century? What import and implications do they hold, particularly when viewing them from a theo-ethical perspective? I contend that spirituals are important for five specific reasons:

1. Spirituals provide a direct link musically, emotionally, and psychologically to Mother Africa.
2. Spirituals offer a glimpse of African cosmological views that informed our ancestors' spirituality/ies.
3. Spirituals serve as reminder and affirmation of the Creator's ultimate authority.
4. Spirituals remind us of the importance of communal spirituality.
5. Spirituals teach us that all emotions are welcome in worship.

A Direct Link

Spirituals remind us that *AfricansinAmerica* created the first original American music, deeded to us by ancestors who carried in their bellies and throats the chants, melodies, and rhythms of Mother Africa. Though there were infinite peoples from differing tribes, countries, and regions of Africa, there were commonalities in the music that was sung and played which survived the Maafa. These include:

- Use of African chants, musical modes, scales, and harmonies
- Dialogical participation, also known as call-and-response

- Improvisation and embellishment of melodies, harmonies, rhythms, and texts
- Rhythmic syncopation, instrumentally and vocally
- Storytelling/folklore in lyrics

Spirituals were not created initially as musical compositions for public performance, but grew from the field hollers, moans, and shouts of those who gave utterance to the pain and joy they bore in work, reflection, and worship. From these experiences, three main categories of spirituals emerged: 1) slow, sustained melodies, 2) call-and-response chants, and 3) syncopated, segmented melodies.[11] As spirituals moved from forests and brush arbors into churches and academic institutions, many of them evolved melodically and harmonically and were codified into arranged compositions that stand as part of the Western choral literature tradition. Creating arranged spirituals served a dual purpose: it standardized certain melodies, preserving them historically under specific song titles and making them universally singable; and it made spirituals more palatable to audiences, giving them an air of respectability as a recognized classical music art form.

However, spirituals in their nascent form not only provided a direct link to Mother Africa musically, but also emotionally and psychologically. To hear the singer inquire, "O Lord, How Come Me Here?," assert, "Sometimes I Feel Like a Motherless Child," or lament, "I'm Just a Poor Wayfaring Stranger," spoke directly to how our ancestors perceived their experiences, and the doubt and despair they felt because the God of their ancestors had allowed them to come to such a pass. Spirituals such as "Ain't-A That Good News," "Ride On, King Jesus," "Done Made My Vow to the Lord," and "City Called Heaven" combined a reality of an unknown future with an eschatological hope in the ultimate victory of good over evil, of liberation over oppression, and the triumph of eternal justice over unrighteousness. To sing spirituals was to give voice to the pain, sorrow, and even mitigated joy that was inherent in the psyches of our African and African American ancestors.

11. Work, "Negro Spiritual," 1:22.

The Significance of Spirituals

A Glimpse of African Cosmological Views

The first *AfricansinAmerica* espoused cosmological views that informed their theo-ethical perspectives about daily conditions of enslavement and were expressed through the theo-ethical statements of belief in the spirituals. *AfricansinAmerica* lived within a cosmological construct that affirmed belief in and personal and communal relation to a supreme deity. This construct included a relational and communal sense of being with all creation, borne of ancestral concepts of divinity. These concepts of divinity included an understanding that all creation, including humanity, is imbued with the Divine, which came into direct conflict with what African-descended persons heard in slave owners' churches. According to the slave owners' preacher, *AfricansinAmerica* were less than human, savages, barbarians, destined to be slaves because of the accursed Ham, and instructed by the apostle Paul to "obey their masters." But because of their understanding of the Divine, enslaved persons recognized these words to be false and unjust. The lyrics of spirituals remind us that, regardless of what words might be spoken about *AfricansinAmerica*, the same God who created the universe created us and pronounced us "good."

Cosmologically, our ancestors also believed in a just God who served as protector, defender, judge, and potential liberator. For Africans, God was intimately concerned with and a major participant in their quest for justice and liberation who rewarded or punished rightly those who perpetrated good or evil on others. Spirituals that proclaimed, "Go Down, Moses," "Mary, Don't You Weep," "Didn't My Lord Deliver Daniel," and "Wade in the Water" affirmed their belief in God's ultimate justice for God's people. They understood Jesus as God's divine representative, a suffering servant and sacrificial lamb who bore physical torture and death because of evil systems of oppression, but, through resurrection, overcame and defeated those systems, not just for himself, but for all who followed his way. When they sang, "Sweet Little Jesus Boy," "Calvary," and "I Want Jesus to Walk with Me," *AfricansinAmerica* affirmed that Jesus identified with and stood in solidarity with the poor, the dispossessed, and the downtrodden. Songs like "Every Time I Feel the Spirit," "The Old Ark's A-Moverin,"and "I've Got Peace Like a River," spoke of their understandings of how the Spirit of God moved in, over, and through them to comfort and empower them to persevere and overcome trials and hardships.

A Reminder of God's Ultimate Authority

When they were brought to North American shores, our ancestors were stripped of every facet of their humanity—the God-given right of freedom, their homelands, families, languages, spiritual and religious rituals and traditions, and names. They were deprived of and forbidden to exhibit any personal or communal authority they might have had over their individual personhood or communal identities. Their days were prescribed and structured, their daily tasks assigned and overseen by others who violently wielded power over them. Spirituals emerged out of these contexts, in part, as a way to express beliefs that God was the ultimate judge and authority, and that, even in the midst of having to comply with malicious earthly rulers, they could practice a form of spiritual disobedience, trusting God to have the final word. Our ancestors faced terrible treatment, horrific and inhumane cruelty; spirituals gave voice to this cruelty, without giving way to despondency. Even in the most poignant of spirituals lies a thread of hope, however slender. In this twenty-first century, rife with oppression, unjust and corrupt abuses of power, voter suppression and election tampering, a daily assault on the rights of the weak and marginalized, spirituals have the power to offer that same slender thread of hope.

A Reminder of Communal Spirituality

African cosmological worldviews were clear that humanity was divinely linked with all creation and therefore had a responsibility to live in communal harmony and accountability. Spirituals communicated this worldview of kinship, asserting that "All God's

The Significance of Spirituals

Chillun Got Shoes," "He's Got the Whole World in His Hands," and "Children, We All Shall Be Free." Though individuals might have been from differing nations, tribes, or peoples, there was a concerted effort to communicate with one another, to learn each other's languages and customs, and to derive a sense of togetherness. Spirituals were a way of calling the community forth to work and worship as one, to overcome manufactured divisions that would keep them separate and weak, and to empower them to press forward. In our contemporary world, spirituals provide an ancestral foundation for twenty-first-century *AfricansinAmerica* struggling with the Eurocentric ideal of individualism. Spirituals remind us that sin and evil arise from communal separation, not a religious laundry list of dos and don'ts. As historian Lawrence Levine reminds us,

> Slave music confronts us with evidence which indicates that, however seriously the slave system may have diminished the central community that had bound African societies together, it was never able to destroy it totally or to leave the individual atomized and psychically defenseless.[12]

All Emotions Are Appropriate

Spirituals, like the ancient psalms, cover the gamut of human emotions. While many spirituals performed in concert halls and on school programs today are those that convey a victorious outcome, historically, spirituals were sung extemporaneously and improvisationally. The themes and meanings of spirituals spoke directly to the needs and desires for expression and communication among enslaved Africans and their descendants.[13] Our ancestors would raise spirituals that spoke to whatever emotions they were experiencing in a particular moment, whether it was anguish, anger, despair, grief, anticipation, or joy. Songs such as "Oh, Freedom," "Nobody Knows the Trouble I've Seen," "Ain't Got Time to Die,"

---

12. Levine, *Black Culture*, 33.
13. Costen, *In Spirit and in Truth*, 41.

"Deep River," "Here's One," "I'm Troubled in Mind," "I Shall Not Be Moved," "Buked and Scorned," and "Glory, Glory, Hallelujah (Since I Laid My Burdens Down)" gave voice to the groanings too deep for words. No emotion was taboo to express, nothing too despondent or too joyous to be lifted in song; our ancestors knew and acknowledged that what mattered was the authenticity of our testimony.

Keeping Spirituals Alive in Contemporary Contexts

Though we will examine the preservation of ancestral sacred music in a later chapter, we cannot overstate the question, "How important then, is it that we keep spirituals alive?" If spirituals remind us that our ancestors knew and believed in God as ultimate authority, knew and believed that they were created persons of worth and dignity, that we were and are called to live together in beloved community, and that the music created by our ancestors is the original American art form, doesn't it behoove us as twenty-first-century *AfricansinAmerica* to ensure that the music keeps on playing? The onus is, indeed, on us, to program and perform spirituals, not once a year during February, but every month of every year, and to make it part and parcel of our lived experiences, as did our ancestors. Spirituals should be heard regularly in our faith communities, schools, institutions of higher learning, and at the meetings of our community and social organizations. They should be the subject of papers, reports, speeches, and other research designed to instruct and inform *AfricansinAmerica* from all educational and socioeconomic levels. We should advocate to hear spirituals sung and discussed on radio, television, and internet programs of national and international scope. Spirituals were born out of the desire to express what *AfricansinAmerica* knew and believed to be true. We have a responsibility in the twenty-first century to examine and illumine what we continue to know and believe to be true.

4

Hymnody in Black

I know I am a child of God
although I move so slow
I'll wait until the Spirit comes
and move at God's command.
—*TRADITIONAL CHANT*

ORIGINS OF AMERICAN HYMNODY

EILEEN SOUTHERN STATES IN her book *The Music of Black Americans* that "colonial society in the seventeenth century was basically a rural society, its music, primarily vocal, organized in relation to the needs of the meetinghouse (or church), the home, and the community."[1] Professional and amateur musicians, both indentured servants and enslaved persons, black and white, served in musical capacities. During this time, American hymnody emerged from psalm singing or psalm lining, a practice that originated in England. A precentor led the singing by chanting one or two lines

1. Southern, *Music of Black Americans*, 25.

at a time, and the congregation responded by singing those same lines. In the northern colonies, Africans, or "Negroes," as they were called, were allowed to worship in Anglo churches, singing from designated pews, separate from whites. The churches of this time, primarily Presbyterian, Reformed, or Congregationalist, engaged in psalm singing or psalm lining. Psalm singing required a song leader, the precentor, to tune the psalm, chanting one or two lines at a time, ending on a definite pitch, and the congregation responding with the singing of the same line. Though they sat in separate pews, Blacks learned the tunes and lyrics as well as whites, and sang them together at many communal events, such as weekly prayer meetings, weddings, funerals and public ceremonies such as Election Day. Organizations such as the Society for the Propagation of the Gospel in Foreign Parts and the Established Church of England sent clergy to convert enslaved Africans to Christianity, and, in some sense, educate them, particularly in religious instruction. Psalm singing was part of the catechetical enterprise. In 1726, the rector of Trinity Church observed that over one hundred English and Negro servants attended the catechism on Sundays and sang psalms at the close of instruction. In the South, some enslaved Africans were allowed to worship in the slaveholders' churches, sitting in balconies or on the floor, or holding separate services at the church.

The 1730s brought the First Great Awakening, a revival movement in the colonies, focused on evangelism, personal piety, and revitalization of church worship. With this revitalization came the need for livelier music, as many felt the common way of singing psalms was grave and too slow. Reformers advocated for "regular singing" using established rules of Western classical music. Many songs used for camp meetings were written by Dr. Isaac Watts, an Anglican cleric who, in 1707, published the book *Hymns and Spiritual Songs*, which gained great popularity with Blacks and whites. Part of their appeal, Melva Costen tells us, was attributed to "(1) use of uncomplicated metrical systems; (2) simplicity of vocabulary; and (3) frequent use of repetition." Also appealing was Watts's concept of hymnody and congregational praise which called for "original expressions of praise, thanksgiving, devotion, and desire for spiritual renewal."[2] This philosophy of hymnody allowed Blacks and whites to feel freer in worship, and thus, more emotionally connected.

Developing alongside psalm singing, hymn lining became a tradition in Black worshiping contexts. Though psalm singing involved lining out a hymn, the precentor lined out the written or remembered tune and the congregation repeated what had been sung. Because this call-and-response style mirrored African retentions of call-and-response, Blacks adapted psalm lining in their own contexts, but with decidedly different African melodic and harmonic tones. Named *Dr. Watts's hymns*, in homage to the composer, this style of singing was performed without accompaniment and required a song leader who lined out the hymn, but in a sort of vocal recitation rather than melodic line. The congregation surged in to respond with a lengthy melodic line, generally employing the pentatonic scale of African chant and harmonies on the fourth or fifth note of that scale. Using the terms common meter, long meter, and short meter, which meant something different in this context than originally intended, Blacks added their own melodies and harmonies to the psalm lining tradition, creating a new musical and liturgical form and style which exists to this day.

In the late 1700s and early 1800s came a Second Great Awakening, a revival movement much like the first, but located primarily among America's frontier towns. At the center of this movement was an evangelical theology based in personal experience and responsibility for initiating one's own religious conversion. Because this iteration of the crusade happened in isolated frontier towns, Blacks and whites of every Protestant denomination, and even some Native Americans, were involved and caught up in the fervor and frenzy of revivalism. At the center of this campaign was the camp meeting, "a continuous religious service spread out over several days, often an entire week, taking place in forests or woods

---

2. Costen, *In Spirit and in Truth*, 44.

under large tents."³ James Goff records in his book *Close Harmony: A History of Southern Gospel*,

> No camp meeting achieved a greater legacy than the Cane Ridge Camp Meeting begun in 1801 in Bourbon County, Kentucky. Planned by Presbyterians as a communitywide communion service, it drew crowds of over 10,000 attendees and became famous for the emotional freedom that many worshippers demonstrated as they shouted and danced under the influence of religious power.⁴

Southern records that "the camp meeting was primarily an interracial institution; indeed, sometimes there were more black worshipers present than white,"⁵ although seating was often segregated. Occasionally, Black ministers would preach at the camp meetings, often drawing thousands of worshipers, Black and white. John Goff notes that some camp meetings established segregated services, but even in segregated meetings Blacks and whites in the South greatly influenced each other, in embracing a more unrestrained worship style and sharing the enthusiastic singing of common hymnody. Historian Albert Raboteau describes this religious mutuality, particularly of the Protestant revivalist tradition, stating,

> Religion, especially the revivalistic, inward, experientially oriented religion to which many slaves and masters adhered had an egalitarian tendency which occasionally led to moments of genuine religious mutuality, whereby Blacks and whites preached to, prayed for, and converted each other in situations where the status of master and slave was, at least for the moment, suspended. In the fervor of religious worship, master and slave, white and Black, could be found sharing a common event, professing a common faith and experiencing a common ecstasy.⁶

A stunning result of these camp meetings was the phenomenal growth experienced by Methodist, Baptist, and Presbyterian

---

3. Southern, *Music of Black Americans*, 82.
4. Goff, *Close Harmony*, 17–18.
5. Southern, *Music of Black Americans*, 83.
6. Raboteau, *Slave Religion*, 314.

denominations during this time. Southern Presbyterians, who numbered 20,000 in 1790, saw a membership exceeding 160,000 by 1835. Baptist churches grew from 40,000 members to almost 300,000, and the ranks of the Methodist Episcopal Church South, which had separated from the Anglican Church in the 1780s, swelled from 40,000 in 1790 to over a million members by 1865, reaching five million members, Black and white, by 1890.

Another result of the development of spiritual songs in these camp meetings was the rise of white and Black singing schools which emerged to train singers in the standard Western musical tradition, using a system of letters called solfege, solmization, or *fasola*. The shape-note singing system made note reading easily attainable by the masses. There were even Black singing school masters, including Newport Gardner, who founded the African Benevolent Society for the education of Black children and was one of the founders of the Colored Union Church in Newport, Rhode Island. The teaching of shape-note singing offered the opportunity for average, everyday rural people to sing hymns and brought yet another air of revival (and some contend a Third Great Awakening), while creating a new market for instructional manuals, songbooks, and other printed music. Collections of these songs met with some immediate commercial success, particularly the most popular collection, *The Sacred Harp*, published in 1844 by Benjamin Franklin White. Some music teachers rejected the shape-note system, deeming it a "dumbing down" of the traditional Western choral tradition. At the root of some of the criticism of shape-note singing was its association with rural or common folk, which evinced itself in a class conflict between them and the educated elite, who felt a need for acquiring traditional music training and skills.

Though Sacred Harp and other singing school traditions were frequented by predominantly white crowds, Blacks also participated where racial segregation did not prevent their attendance, and some created their own communities, such as the "Wiregrass Singers" in southeast Alabama. Judge Jackson, a Black self-educated Alabama farmer, compiled and published the book *The Colored*

Sacred Harp, which, though patterned after the original *Sacred Harp*, he viewed as a vehicle used to incorporate a cultural expression of his own making. At the Smithsonian Institution's 1970 Festival of American Folklife, Dewey Williams, a Black singing school teacher and Sacred Harp enthusiast, led the Sacred Harp presentations, along with his white colleague, Hugh McGrath. Though there was initial tension among the singers, by the third day of the festival, admiration for Mr. Williams had replaced aloofness. One white attendee remarked,

> It's the Negroes who are making this go, not us. We sing it so straight it nearly breaks, but you've got to mix a little of the rock and roll and give the people what they like. When we first came up here, we kinda turned up our noses at Dewey, but now we're kinda taking off our hats to him. We talk about having the Spirit with Sacred Harp: Well, he has it.[7]

Much like the camp meetings of the Second Great Awakening, the highlight of these gatherings was the dissemination of new "convention songs" called *gospel songs*, because they were not traditional or orthodox hymns. Like the "spiritual songs" of the camp meetings, many of these gospel song writers added new choruses to established hymns or created completely new gospel hymns by borrowing melodies from popular songs and tunes of the day, giving them sacred lyrics and adding catchy refrains. Three of the most significant proponents of this new music were Dwight Lyman Moody, a layman associated with the YMCA in Chicago, Ira Sankey, and Mrs. Alexander Van Alstyne, better known to the public as Fanny Crosby, who wrote "Blessed Assurance," "I Am Thine, O Lord," "Near the Cross," "Pass Me Not, O Gentle Savior," and "All the Way My Savior Leads Me." A singer/songwriter from Pennsylvania, Moody felt his calling was to preach the gospel and Sankey felt his to sing the gospel. In fact, Sankey is generally given credit for linking the term "gospel" to religious music because of the popularity he and Moody enjoyed in England and because

---

7. Boyd, *Judge Jackson*, 96–97.

of Sankey's publication *Gospel Hymns and Sacred Songs* in 1875. Other composers, such as Phillip Bliss, James Rowe, and William Bradbury wrote enduring favorites such as "Wonderful Words of Life," "It Is Well with My Soul," "'Tis So Sweet to Trust in Jesus," "Love Lifted Me," "Jesus Loves Me, This I Know," "Just as I Am," "Sweet Hour of Prayer," and "The Solid Rock."

HYMNODY IN BLACK PROTESTANT CHURCHES

By the 1890s, many Black Christians had left predominantly white churches and formed their own denominations. In the North, clergymen like Richard Allen and Absalom Jones began African Methodist and Episcopal congregations. In the South, the Colored Methodist Episcopal (CME) Church was formed,[8] and Black Baptist churches were springing up, creating a network of connectivity called conventions. Pentecostal, Holiness, Apostolic, and Sanctified denominations also arose following the Azusa Street Revival of 1906. Part and parcel of most Black denominations was a commitment to effectual and fervent worship, lively singing and, for some, ecstatic shouting. According to music scholar and historian Portia Maultsby, Allen "chose to establish a form of worship based on the aesthetic and cultural reference of his Black congregation, modifying the Methodist worship style to accommodate his congregation and reshaping the musical tradition of the Methodists."[9] He solved the issue of inadequate access to a canon of song for his distinct congregation by publishing in 1801 a collection of hymns, titled *A Collection of Spiritual Songs and Hymns Selected from Various Authors by Richard Allen, African Minister*. Allen's hymnal contained fifty-four hymn texts, without tunes, drawn mostly from the hymns of Dr. Watts and Wesley, but also included hymns popular with Baptists. Though Allen's first hymnal preceded the development of the "gospel" hymn, Allen also is credited with the practice

---

8. The name "Colored Methodist Episcopal Church" was changed to "Christian Methodist Episcopal Church" in 1954.

9. Maultsby, "Use and Performance," 1:85.

of adding a refrain to hymn texts, at will, a form of improvisation which infused informality in the worship service. Early hymnals of other Black denominations, including African Methodist Episcopal Zion (AMEZ), CME, and Black Baptist churches often utilized material previously printed for white denominations, but intentionally included popular gospel hymns of the day.

Though wanting to keep some of the hymns and choruses of African and Black traditions, the composers and compilers of hymnody in these Black denominations, particularly the Methodist bodies, steered clear of emotional and ecstatic expressions in worship. Many of these Black worshiping congregations imitated the solemn, cultured style of the Euro/Anglo congregations they had previously experienced, and their hymnody reflected this style. Other early Black Methodist hymnals included Peter Spence's 1822 *Union African Hymnbook*, and the AMEZ hymnal, *Hymns for the Use of the American Methodist Episcopal Zion Church*, published in 1838. One of the first, and perhaps most well-loved, hymnals for use by Black Baptists was *Gospel Pearls*, published in 1921 by the Sunday School Publishing Board of the National Baptist Convention, USA. It enjoyed enduring popularity because it included metered/lined hymns and beloved gospel hymnody of both Euro/Anglo and Black composers.[10] Other hymnals specifically compiled for use primarily by Black Protestant congregations include *The New National Baptist Hymnal*, published in 1977; *Songs of Zion*, a 1981 publication of the United Methodist Church; *Yes, Lord!* published by the Church of God in Christ in 1982; and most recently, the *African American Heritage Hymnal* published by GIA in 2001. *Songs of Zion*, *Yes, Lord!*, and the *African American Heritage Hymnal* each contain an extensive compilation of African American sacred genres of music, including spirituals, lined hymns and/or chants that have been transcribed, and traditional and contemporary gospel songs, making these hymnals extremely useful for congregations who desire to sing a variety of genres each week without having to purchase multiple sets of hymnals.

---

10. We will engage a fuller discussion of gospel hymnody as a precursor to gospel music in ch. 5.

Hymnody in Black

What have hymns meant to Black worshiping congregations? Wendell Whalum wrote that African American hymnody is

> all serious music that is sacred to the Black experience ... and all the serious music that falls within the boundaries of Christianity as it seized the Black experience as well as that serious music which was sacred to the experience, but not necessarily Christian in nature.[11]

Hymns are dear to the Black church because encapsulated within them are many of the first Christian statements of faith our ancestors heard that rang true to them. Before our ancestors knew the words "theology" or "affirmation of faith," they heard lyrics such as "Father, I stretch my hands to Thee, no other help I know / if Thou withdraw Thyself from me, oh wither shall I go," "I love the Lord, He heard my cry and pitied every groan / Long as I live and troubles rise, I'll hasten to His throne," and "A charge to keep I have, a God to glorify / A never-dying soul to save and fit it for the sky." These lyrics struck at the heart of enslaved Africans and their descendants, as well as free women and men of color, giving voice to the daily struggles and sorrows they endured in a foreign land that did not embrace them or their heritage. The theologies contained in songs like "What a Friend We Have in Jesus," "Blessed Assurance," "I Sing the Mighty Power of God," and "O God, Our Help in Ages Past" resonated with what Africans and African Americans knew and had been taught about God through their forebears. Cosmologies and theologies from the African continent included beliefs in one supreme God, sacred cosmos, divine relationality, and communal relatedness in the form of kinship. Many of these beliefs were echoed in the lyrics to hymns sung in colonial churches, both northern and southern, and independent Black churches that sprang up after emancipation. Further, these hymns were used as teaching tools in Black churches for the purposes of Christian spiritual formation. Doctrinal tenets were explained through hymn lyrics in songs like "Holy, Holy, Holy," "The Church's One Foundation," "At the Cross," and "Because He Lives." Worshipers who would never step foot in

---

11. Whalum, "Black Hymnody," 1:168.

a seminary could grasp concepts like the Trinitarian nature of God, eschatology, soteriology, ecclesiology, and sanctification through the singing of hymns.

The singing of hymns also reminded early Black worshiping congregations of their communal identity. Until the mid-1900s, the majority of Black churches met biweekly, as most ordained clergy served a circuit comprised of several churches spread over a particular geographic area. On the Sundays when a particular church did not convene for worship, their congregants often visited other neighborhood churches, regardless of denomination. While doctrinal tenets and liturgies might have differed somewhat, the music for most of these congregations was very similar. Hymns with easily sung melodies and harmonies became favorites among Black congregations and would have been readily recognized and heartily sung by most participants. This experience further underscored the communal identity of those attending, both as Black and Christian. Hymns such as "Oh, How I Love Jesus," "Great Is Thy Faithfulness," "Yes, God Is Real," and "The Lord Will Make a Way Somehow" were well known within Black Christian worshiping communities and became musical standards that remain to this day. Church musicians and worship leaders were and are expected to know how to play, sing, and lead these standards, regardless of what contemporary hymns, praise choruses, or top-forty gospel hits may be popular.

CONTEMPORARY ISSUES

Though hymnody has been part of the Black Christian worshiping experience for centuries, contemporary usage of hymns has declined in many churches for various reasons, including negative perspectives on hymn usage, generational gaps in teaching and learning hymns, and dearth/scarcity of musicians proficient in hymnody. We will explore each of these circumstances below.

Hymnody in Black

Negative Perspectives on Hymnody

Why aren't churches singing hymns anymore? Well, many still are, but a vast number of others are not. As a seminary professor, I've had extensive opportunities to ask students who serve Christian congregations about the music performed in their churches. When the subject of hymnody arises, many students remark that hymnody is not relevant in their worshiping contexts, particularly if they serve churches established within the last twenty years. With the advent of gospel music in the 1950s and praise choruses in the 1960s, both of which have made enormous impacts on worship in the twentieth and twenty-first centuries and are still evolving into multiple genres and styles, hymnody has often been pushed to the side in worship, if not pushed out altogether. Why have congregations gravitated toward these other genres and styles to the diminishment of hymnody? Many pastors and musicians have shared with me that their congregations find hymnody too traditional, stuffy, staid, and boring, preferring instead the more modern sounds of gospel and praise music. Congregants, especially younger members, complain about difficulty in singing hymns with tunes that are pitched too high, tempos that are too slow, and lyrics that employ antiquated and even offensive language. Further, in this day of a more educated citizenry, members often point out troublesome theologies and histories that underlie many well-loved traditional hymns.

Generational Gaps in Hymn Singing

Another issue with singing hymns is the loss of musical inheritance across generations. Several generational gaps have occurred in the worship attendance in most churches over the past fifty years. No longer is the family group attendance paradigm the norm in worship; instead, there is more individual attendance, which, in some ways, has resulted in a break in the passage of knowledge from generation to generation regarding liturgy and music in worship. Many people attend churches where, initially, they were unfamiliar with the rituals, words, and music used in worship. They did not attend church weekly as children or grandchildren where an adult modeled ways of worship for them. Thus, they were not steeped in church worshiping traditions, nor did they learn church music. For those now attending churches that still employ traditional hymnody, many are at a loss when it comes to participating in liturgy and music, particularly the singing of hymns. This, in turn, has led to many churches using more well-known contemporary music, to the marginalization of hymnody. Churches that employ less or nontraditional liturgies and music rarely sing hymns in worship services, preferring instead to program gospel music and praise choruses throughout, in congregational and ensemble singing. Many of these contexts are newer congregations that do not have denominational or historic ties to traditional hymnody. While pastors, worship leaders, and even members of these churches may be familiar with hymns, they do not see a need for hymnody in worship, and some even contend that singing hymns is more off-putting than welcome among worship attendees.

Dearth of Church Musicians

One last cause of declining hymn singing in worship is the scarcity of musicians who can play hymns well. Decades ago, it was common practice for children, female and male, to take piano lessons. Piano teachers who offered inexpensive lessons were in great supply and many schools and churches even offered affordable piano instruction. Further, schools and churches offered opportunities for children to play in public, in recitals, musicals, plays, and other events. In the past fifteen to twenty years, however, this has not been the case. Private piano instruction is difficult to secure in many cities, and if an instructor is located the cost can be prohibitive. The paradigm of school music teachers who doubled as church musicians and private piano teachers has changed drastically, if not disappeared completely. There have been two unfortunate outcomes of this shift: 1) significant numbers of children are not learning piano or other keyboard instruments; and 2) churches no longer have a substantive pool of musicians from which to hire for worship services.

Hymnody in Black

When large numbers of children were learning piano, many of them were not only being taught the rudiments of classical music, but many, like me, were also learning church music, including hymnody. I was blessed to have as my first significant piano teacher the same person who directed and accompanied our church choir. Therefore, my lessons were filled with Bach, Beethoven, Brahms, and Bradbury (William); I played Chopin, Clementi, and Crosby (Fanny), as well as Tchaikovsky, Telemann, and Tindley (Charles). In fact, all her students who attended churches were required to learn (and sight-read) hymns. She told us, "Churches are always looking for good musicians and knowing how to play hymns will serve you well." She was not the only piano teacher who stressed being able to play hymns, and many church musicians, even today, will tell you they first learned to play, or had their first opportunity to play in public, in church. Now, however, it is rare to find affordable, private piano instruction that has a church music component included. Further, because gospel music and praise choruses have become so prevalent in worship services, many musicians taking piano lessons in the last two decades failed to see the value in learning to play hymns, so that was not part of their musical training. In fact, many musicians now are claiming to be self-taught and do not read music, which also hinders them from learning hymnody.

As a result of the lack of church music teaching and training, many churches are left without fully proficient musicians to serve in worship. I use the qualifier "fully" because musicians may be able to play quite well genres and styles of music that do not require music reading, but are unable to play hymns, anthems, cantatas, and other scored church music. This generally limits the church's musical repertoire to one or two genres of music, and results in fewer, if any, hymns being sung in worship, or the same few hymns being sung week after week, which hampers the church's musical growth. The lack of teaching and training has also resulted in many churches employing musicians who are unable to provide the quality of music the church desires. There are congregations who would sing a wider variety of hymns, but the scant availability of musicians prevents being able to perform them.

5

The Emergence and Evolution of Gospel Music

> *It's a feeling within; you can't help yourself. I don't know; it goes between my marrow and my bones. It just makes you feel like . . . you heard me say I wanna fly away somewhere? I feel like I can fly away! I forget I'm in the world sometimes, just wanna take off.*
>
> —Mother Willie Mae Ford Smith[1]

GOSPEL MUSIC ROOTS

THE MUSIC WHICH CAME to be known as *gospel* had several points of origin. One was the gospel hymnody that evolved from the aforementioned camp meetings of the Great Awakenings of the eighteenth and nineteenth centuries. Even more than the preaching, the most exciting part of the camp meeting was the singing. There were no separate groups performing or alternating hymns or tunes, as on a program. Everyone sang hymns together, those

---

1. Interview with Mother Smith in Nierenberg, *Say Amen, Somebody*.

The Emergence and Evolution of Gospel Music

written by Watts, Charles and John Wesley, and other popular hymn writers of the time. They would sing for a great length of time, and even after the day was over, Black attendees could be heard in their segregated quarters singing through the night. As Swedish novelist Fredrika Bremer, a visitor to one such camp meeting, observed, "On the black side of the camp the tents were still full of religious exaltation, each separate tent presenting some new phasis, in one tent a song of the spiritual Canaan was being sung excellently, at half past five the next morn, the hymns of the Negroes were still to be heard on all sides."[2] Shared between Black and white attendees were the African retentions of syncopated rhythms, melodies, and call-and-response styles which would thread their way into future music genres of both races. Another influence of Blacks, perceived negatively by some white attendees, was the addition of refrains and choruses, prayers and Scriptures, to the orthodox hymns, some almost sounding like the dance tune of jubilee dance melodies. Though some saw this practice as anathema, it would continue and grow into a new form of music known as the camp meeting hymn.

Akin to the livelier hymnody necessitated by the First Great Awakening, the Second Great Awakening produced a new hymnody, developed to meet the needs of a mostly illiterate congregation, seeking catchier tunes than what they perceived to be the outdated hymnody of England. Song leaders added choruses and refrains with repetitive phrases to established hymns, even composing songs on the spot. These new songs, inspired by the extemporaneous singing of Black attendees and constructed from popular folk melodies, would be called *spiritual songs*, distinguishing them from psalms and hymns. Goff also notes the development of these spiritual songs, stating that

> choruses were popular for several reasons. They tended to be catchy tunes easy to sing and learn. They were constructed from popular folk melodies already well known

---

2. Southern, *Music of Black Americans*, 84.

to many in the audience and they solved the dual problem of illiteracy and a shortage of songbooks.[3]

As mentioned in chapter 4, proponents of this evolving style would link the new music with conversion theology and Evangelicalism, creating a new genre of gospel hymnody. Gospel hymns would become extremely important to the congregational music of both white and Black denominations and to the ultimate evolution into *gospel* music as a genre.

A second point of origin was the rise of independent Black churches in northern American cities during the Great Migration of the early to mid-1900s. Many northern mainline denominational Black congregations, particularly those deemed "silk-stocking" churches, imitated the austere, demure style of white congregations. However, Black migrants who had come to the North seeking a better life, finding instead unemployment, inadequate housing, and sometimes the same racial hostility and violence they left in the South, refused to alter their worship practices, and instead created or joined Sanctified[4] churches, sometimes identified with the phrase holiness-Pentecostal. Scholar Cheryl Sanders states, "The Sanctified church is closely related to three distinct Old and New World religious traditions: African religion, White 'protest Protestantism' and Haitian vaudou."[5] Two distinct characteristics of Pentecostal worship made it attractive to Blacks: the emotional nature of worship and that it was essentially a religion of the socially underprivileged. For the most part, Pentecostals came from lower socioeconomic levels and might have experienced marginalization in traditional denominations. A further draw for the church was the fact that educational standards for the ministry were almost nonexistent.

---

3. Goff, *Close Harmony*, 18.

4. "The label *Sanctified church* distinguished these congregations of saints from other Black Christians, especially those identified as Baptist or Methodist who assimilated and imitated the cultural and organizational models of European-American patriarchy." Sanders, "In the World," 1:100.

5. Sanders, "In the World," 1:99.

The Emergence and Evolution of Gospel Music

The exuberant style of worship in these congregations was mirrored by the white holiness-Pentecostal congregations. Hymnals written for these congregations include Charles Price Jones's *Sweet Selections* and *Jesus Only Standard Hymnal*. Goff asserts,

> The fact is that both white and black Christians affiliated with the Holiness-Pentecostal wing of Protestantism found much to shout about in their worship services and those emotions spilled logically over into their singing. The roots of gospel music are found in the rural churches that routinely failed to conform to the more sophisticated style of their urban counterparts.[6]

A third root of gospel can be found in the music that infused the worship of these urban churches and denominations, including the Church of God in Christ (COGIC), established by Charles Harrison Mason after he was introduced to Pentecostal teachings and practices while participating in the Azusa Street Revival.[7] Two Black gospel hymn writers whose music would be essential to the development of the gospel tradition in the COGIC and other denominations were Charles A. Tindley and Thomas A. Dorsey.

Rev. Charles Albert Tindley migrated to Philadelphia from his birth state of Maryland after the Civil War. Though not formally educated, Tindley was exceptionally intelligent, mastering both Hebrew and Greek languages and becoming ordained in the Methodist Episcopal Church in 1887. He is considered the "pivotal force in the development of composed and published African American gospel songs."[8] Tindley did not intend his compositions to be sung in formal worship services, but, rather, composed songs

---

6. Goff, *Close Harmony*, 6.

7. "William Seymour, a Black minister born in Louisiana in 1870 to emancipated parents, grew up observing brush arbor worship syncretized with Creole religious practices. After joining the Holiness Church, and influenced by the teachings of Charles Parham, an early Pentecostal minister, Seymour moved to Los Angeles and initiated the Azusa Street Revival, a Pentecostal movement that grew into a historic nine-year revival attended weekly by thousands of people from across the country." Allen, *Womanist Theology of Worship*, 207.

8. Costen, *In Spirit and in Truth*, 82.

for Sunday schools, prayer meetings, and social gatherings. His gospel hymnody, a style of song that used imagery to interpret oppression faced by African Americans and encouraged believers to have faith in God until the storm had passed, would serve as a precursor to traditional gospel music. Rev. Tindley wrote and published these songs in his hymn collections, *Soul Echoes* (1905) and *New Songs of Paradise* (1916), the latter of which included "I'll Overcome Someday" which would become the anthem of the civil rights movement fifty years later.[9]

Dr. Thomas A. Dorsey, a former blues and honky-tonk keyboard player who was influenced by Rev. Tindley and was the first to give gospel music its name, is considered the father of traditional gospel music. Dorsey set spiritual/sacred lyrics to blues tunes and called it "gospel." He then collaborated with female singers to perform his tunes, including Roberta Martin, Sallie Martin, Mother Willie Mae Ford Smith, and, perhaps his most famous partner of all, Mahalia Jackson. Many of the tunes he composed became known by the women who performed and recorded them, becoming identified by African American women as powerful anthems of inspiration, protest, and/or solace. Songs such as "Precious Lord," "I'm Going to Live the Life I Sing About," "If You See My Savior," "Peace in the Valley," "It's a Highway to Heaven," and "The Lord Will Make a Way Somehow" spoke not only to the plight, but the faith of African American women. In 1933, Dorsey founded the National Convention of Choirs and Choruses, which attracted choirs and soloists from all over the country. Other composers followed Dorsey's lead and gospel soon grew to greater heights, inspiring such groups as the Clara Ward Singers, Dr. Mattie Moss Clark and the Clark Sisters, and the Caravans, which included gospel greats Albertina Walker, Dorothy Norwood, and Reverend Shirley Caesar. One of Dorsey's protégés, the Reverend James Cleveland, ushered gospel into the modern age and founded the Gospel Music Workshop of America, which still meets annually and has chapters across the world. The majority of these choirs, groups, and soloists were and are composed of

---

9. Lincoln and Mamiya, *Black Church*, 360.

African American women, because they were and are the majority of church attendees.

Dorsey's bluesy style caused him to be chastised and even evicted from several churches who felt that gospel was too secular or worldly sounding, regardless of the libretti used. Many felt that the soloistic efforts were too showy and elaborate to be true worship and they believed that the congregation was being entertained rather than spiritually inspired by these efforts. E. Franklin Frazier comments, "Some of the so-called advanced Negro churches resented these gospel singers and refused to permit them to sing within their churches."[10] However, gospel music was the music of the people, "an accommodation between traditional Negro religion and the new outlook of Negroes in the new American environment."[11] As this music began to grow in popularity, not only with Blacks, but whites as well, it became secularized and part of "the attempt of the Negro to utilize his religious heritage in order to come to terms with changes in his own institutions as well as the problems of the world of which he is a part."[12] Gospel music came out of the urban community and claimed its Black identity. It did not try to legitimize itself by associating with white religious music, but, rather, distinguished itself from white music by incorporating those stylistic elements that had been viewed negatively by the white establishment, including many elements that were thought secular—the melodies, rhythms, and motions.[13] It was being used not only for church services or concerts, but for sit-ins and marches as well. As it was adopted by younger people, gospel music continued to evolve into a form that used even more secular rhythms and instrumentation. This has come to be known as *modern* and *contemporary gospel music*.

---

10. Frazier, *Negro Church*, 78.
11. Frazier, *Negro Church*, 77.
12. Frazier, *Negro Church*, 79.
13. Lincoln and Mamiya, *Black Church*, 359–60.

Over My Head
CONTEMPORARY GOSPEL MUSIC

Modern gospel music began in the late 1960s and early 1970s with the invention of the electric organ, modern amplification, and recording. It was included at the 1957 Newport Jazz Festival and soon was featured by radio stations across the country. Singers such as the Walter Hawkins Love Alive Choir, the Andraé Crouch Singers, Rev. James Cleveland, and many others wrote and performed this music to audiences worldwide. As modern gospel continued to evolve, it began to increasingly incorporate spiritual melodies with driving rhythms and percussive beats that were often derived from secular sources. Many of the aforementioned groups began to augment their performances with bass and rhythm guitar, full percussion outfits, and choreography. The music became known as *contemporary gospel* and it would hit the ground running. Its appeal transcends ages, though the primary listening group consists of teenagers and young adults. Many of these groups, including the Hawkins Family, the Clark Sisters, Commissioned, the New Jersey Mass Choir, the Georgia Mass Choir, and Milton Brunson and the Thompson Community Choir have intentionally pushed the boundaries of traditional gospel sound by incorporating elements of rhythm and blues, jazz, and funk music into their accompaniments. While the inclusion of these new elements made gospel appealing to a wider audience, it also caused controversy within churches and even denominations, as it did for Dr. Mattie Moss Clark and the Clark Sisters, whose song "You Brought the Sunshine" reflected the influence of Stevie Wonder's reggae-inspired hit "Master Blaster."

Gospel music of the late twentieth and early twenty-first centuries has retained many of its original musical characteristics, even as it has incorporated a more technologically advanced sound. Computer-generated and AI-enhanced instrumentation, voicing, rhythms, and accompanying videos serve as synthesized foundations to lyrics that, while written in modern vernacular, still attest to God's sovereignty, the love of Jesus, and the power of the Holy Spirit. One group that has been able to navigate

The Emergence and Evolution of Gospel Music

twenty-first-century technological influences while maintaining their gospel roots is the Winans family. Headed by the late David "Pop" Winans and the late Delores "Mom" Winans, the Winans family encompasses several solo artists and groups, including the Winans, Three Winans Brothers, Benjamin (BeBe) and Priscilla (CeCe) Winans, and Bishop Marvin Winans. Many of their recordings and videos reflect musical characteristics and cultural influences of both traditional gospel and popular music and have generated tremendous crossover appeal. Several secular music artists have joined the Winans on recordings, including Anita Baker, Teddy Riley, Aaron Hall of Guy, Take 6, and Whitney Houston, creating a wider audience for the music, resulting in airplay on secular radio stations and television networks, and topping R&B and pop, as well as gospel charts.

Kirk Franklin, one of the most commercially successful gospel music artists in history, dismantled boundaries of traditional gospel sound by sampling secular music into his compositions. His crossover hit "Stomp (Remix)" contains samples of Parliament Funkadelic's "One Nation Under a Groove" and Busta Rhymes's "Woo-Hah!! Got You All in Check," featuring rap lyrics by Salt of the rap duo Salt-N-Pepa. Franklin would go on to sample music of artists such as Biggie Smalls, Patrice Rushen, Bill Withers, and Scarface, continuing to forge new paths over ground that had been uprooted by Rosetta Tharpe, James Cleveland, Edwin and Walter Hawkins, John P. Kee, and other contemporary gospel music pioneers.

As gospel music became more prevalent in African American worship, it grew to be a balm to worshipers, particularly *AfricansinAmerica* who identified and still identify with themes present in gospel music. Gospel songs tell the love of an omnipresent, omniscient, omnipotent God who sent Jesus as liberator, savior, and redeemer and focus on how one's faith and belief in God and/or Jesus will provide help, healing, deliverance, and restoration. Gospel music, from its inception, has reportedly had the power to liberate persons, emotionally, mentally, and spiritually. Gospel pioneer Mother Willie Mae Ford Smith testifies about the power of gospel in the documentary *Say Amen, Somebody*, stating, "It's a feeling within; you can't help yourself. I don't know; it goes between my marrow and my bones. It just makes you feel like . . . you heard me say I wanna fly away somewhere? I feel like I can fly away! I forget I'm in the world sometimes, just wanna take off."[14]

Many composers and artists have commented on the ability of gospel music to draw persons into what they would describe as life-changing encounters with God and/or Jesus. They have asserted that gospel music attracts persons to worship when other elements of worship, including preaching, may not. This author has heard countless remarks from people who continued to attend churches because of stirring choir performances, performances which allowed them to release pent-up emotions and feel a sense of peace. Others note that gospel music speaks to their souls in a way that other sacred music does not; it has a "raw-ness" about it, an authenticity that cannot be captured on paper, but must be felt and experienced. Moreover, gospel music transcends boundaries of generation, denomination, and what is accepted as "sacred." Gospel music, traditional and contemporary, uses musical elements from all genres, including blues, rock, funk, rhythm and blues, and jazz. As long as the lyrics are considered "sacred," it is still considered gospel music. In some cases, the lyrics may not overtly mention God or Jesus but imply that God and/or Jesus are to be credited with the deliverance noted in the song (e.g., "Never Would Have Made It," composed by Pastor Marvin Sapp).

GOSPEL MUSIC MEANING MAKING

What meaning has gospel had historically for *AfricansinAmerica* and does it continue to have this same meaning?

Testimonies of Faith

One of the primary reasons gospel music has been and still is so prevalent in African-descended worshiping communities is

---

14. Interview with Mother Smith in Nierenberg, *Say Amen, Somebody.*

because it provides opportunities for individual and collective testimonies of faith. Early gospel singers gravitated toward this new genre because it gave them a vehicle to give their testimonies in song. Selections such as "If You See My Savior," "Move On Up a Little Higher," "I'll Tell It Wherever I Go," and "May the Work I've Done Speak for Me," are direct reflections of the singer's personal life and witness to their relationship with God. The stories of early gospel greats such as Mahalia Jackson, Mother Willie Mae Ford Smith, Roberta Martin, Sallie Martin, Clara Ward, the Caravans, the O'Neal Twins, and the Barrett Sisters have been documented in books and videos, and throughout each narrative one can hear the dedication, perseverance, and commitment to the calling of spreading the gospel of Jesus Christ through song. Many gospel artists have testified that it was the power of gospel music that brought them to a relationship with God, "rescuing" and "saving" them from bondage to sin. While hymn lyrics often begin with a collective praise to God which can be internalized as individual affirmations, gospel lyrics begin with personal testimonies and move outward (in choruses and refrains) as communal affirmations.

Connection to the Early/Institutional Black Church

As gospel music gained traction and established footholds in Chicago, St. Louis, and other urban areas, solo artists and gospel groups began to record music and perform in revivals and concerts. This allowed the music to be disseminated across the country to larger audiences and brought greater attention to and wider acceptance of gospel music which transcended geographic, denominational, and, eventually, socioeconomic boundaries. Gospel music became an additional unifying factor for Black faith communities, along with commitments to social justice and racial uplift, undergirding the sense of connection and institutional identity of the Black church. As contemporary congregations, artists, and groups continue to sing gospel music, we are reminded of and connected with those early progenitors and creators of the genre, and of the ways gospel music served to connect people and faith communities across boundaries. Every time a gospel standard is performed live or re-recorded, a songwriter arranges or composes gospel music, or a choir director teaches gospel music, the participants and hearers are brought into the presence of those who came before, witnessing to the enduring legacies of their testimonies.

Use of Biblical Narratives

In addition to being purveyors of personal testimonies, gospel music lyrics have also extolled the heroes and heroines of biblical narratives as faith exemplars. Songs like "Mary, Don't You Weep," "If I Perish (I'm Going to See the King)," "Jesus Will Work It Out," "He Never Failed Me Yet," and "He's an On-Time God" retell the stories of those in Scripture whose lives testify to the power, authority, grace, and mercy of a just and liberating God. When our enslaved ancestors were introduced to North American versions of Christianity, it was for the supposed intent of "civilizing" them— addressing their "heathenish" and "barbaric" natures. On the face of it, "Christianizing" enslaved *AfricansinAmerica* was for the benefit of their eternal souls; however, the truth of the matter was slaveholders hoped it would prevent them from revolting against and/or escaping enslavement. Part of the religious indoctrination was preaching and teaching enslaved persons from biblical texts that affirmed slavery and obedience to authority, and interpreting texts in ways that admonished enslaved persons to accept their marginalized status as God ordained. However, even from the antebellum period, many *AfricansinAmerica* knew that what was being preached and taught in the slaveholders' churches was antithetical to their understandings of who God was. They began to worship secretly, in fields, forests, and brush arbors, creating the *invisible institution*, and with it, their own sacred music that affirmed their beliefs in a God of liberation and justice. They sang about biblical heroes and sheroes who fought against oppression and were delivered out of bondage in spirituals such as "Go Down, Moses," "I Got Shoes," "Wade in the Water," and "Didn't My Lord Deliver Daniel."

Gospel music continued that legacy, with lyrics that herald these same freedom fighters empowered by this same God of justice and righteousness. While some music critics would claim gospel music is replete only with pie-in-the-sky end-time theologies, lyrics to the gospel songs mentioned previously tell a different story. For example, the lyrics to "Mary, Don't You Weep" remind the singer and listener that "Pharaoh's army got drowned in the Red Sea," meaning, the ones who thought they had power and authority to marginalize those they deemed weaker were defeated by the God who has all power and authority. Another gospel song that tells a similar story about Moses is "On-Time God," which extols God as the ultimate, right-on-time deliverer, rescuing the Israelites from impending death at the hands of Pharaoh and his armies.[15]

The lyrics to Robert Ray's "He Never Failed Me Yet" also include a reference to Moses, as well as tributes to God's liberating power in the story of the three Hebrew boys delivered from Nebuchadnezzar's furnace.[16] Though these lyrics attest to God's authority and power to move in the lives of biblical characters, what is just as, if not more, important is the assurance that God will do the same for God's people today who find themselves marginalized and oppressed. The choruses of both of these songs focus on how God continues today to rescue and deliver those who ask for and trust in God's divine power.

While the solo lyrics of these and other gospel music songs tell individual stories or personal testimonies, the choruses remind us of the communal nature of God's liberative work in the world. Gospel lyrics remind us that what God has done for others, God will surely do for us.

15. "He's an On-Time God," on Peoples, *On-Time God*.
16. Ray, *He Never Failed Me Yet*.

Provide Avenues for Musical and Lyrical Experimentation

From its inception, gospel music pushed and stretched musical and lyrical boundaries. First, the instrumentation of gospel music moved beyond acoustic piano to electronic and percussion instruments that migrated from nightclubs into churches. Use of Hammond organ, bass and lead guitars, and drum kits helped create the unique sound that is gospel music. Today's gospel music instrumentation goes even further with the use of technology to create an even more contemporary sound. Second, chord structures and rhythmic syncopation of rhythm and blues, jazz, and even rock genres helped distinguish gospel music as a contemporary genre that navigated between what some considered secular music and the more accepted sacred church sound. Third, choirs and ensembles were employed differently in gospel music than with anthems or spirituals. When singing anthems or spirituals, choirs were the featured "artist," while, in gospel, choirs served as the collective musical affirmation to the soloist's assertions and testimonies. In today's gospel music, choirs continue to provide harmonic communal refrains and choruses, collective affirmations sung in unison verses, as well as percussive and melodic accents that evoke current trends in electronic and digital music production. Last, gospel music is one of the foremost sacred genres utilizing improvisation as a musical device. In both solo and instrumental performances, gospel artists employ melodic and rhythmic tools including melismata, trills, scales, arpeggios, repetition, syncopation, and call-and-response as ways to create unique presentations of songs. An artist may perform a song hundreds of times, but uses improvisation to create a sense of newness in each performance.

6

Preserving the Gift of African-Descended Sacred Music in Contemporary Worship

The Spirit will not descend without a song.
—African proverb

Now that we have taken a deep look into the histories and meanings of genres of music that have been employed in African American Christian worship spaces, let's consider how we move forward in worship utilizing these genres. How do we preserve this music, these ancestral gifts and legacies that have infused worship across generations?

One of the ways we preserve the music of our heritage is by knowing as much as we can about it. It is amazing (and unfortunate) to me how little today's Black worshiping congregations seem to know about Black sacred music. Many are unaware of the history of spirituals and Black hymnody, in particular. Growing up, I received historical background each week on the music we sang and played in my home church from our choral director. She would share with us the importance of each genre and of specific songs to our culture and worship context. To do this, of course, meant she had done the research necessary to share the information competently. She had multiple music degrees and was most proficient in music history. Further, when she was preparing to teach a particular genre of music, she always reviewed her research anew, to ensure the information she was sharing was pertinent and included any recent scholarship on the subject. When I became a church choral director, I followed in her footsteps, making sure that I researched the music I was teaching, and shared that research with singers and congregations alike. Often, when I have received initial reticence about performing a particular genre of music or song, my ability to provide historical and musical significance has helped people understand why we were learning and performing said pieces. Sometimes, sharing my research has inspired participants to conduct their own research and share it with others, another crucial outgrowth of research itself as a discipline. I am not suggesting that persons require music degrees to teach this information; I am advocating that they do the research necessary to provide adequate and accurate information that will help singers and instrumentalists connect with and perceive the importance of the music they are learning.

If churches want to preserve this music and see it continue being used in congregational and choral singing, I contend it is vital that those responsible for presenting it conduct the necessary research to understand its importance to our histories and cultures. This means reviewing multiple resources across time about each genre. Reading an encyclopedic synopsis of each genre is not sufficient; one must plumb the depths of resources, both historic and recent, to gain an understanding of and appreciation for how the genre was conceived and how it has developed over time. Spirituals, hymnody, and gospel music each have unique beginnings, the histories of which are essential to know for comprehending their musical sounds, lyrics, and instrumentations. Further, there are decades (and even centuries) of research about these genres which detail their respective evolutions over time and place that are critical to understanding the importance of their continued presence and performance in contemporary worship spaces. It is also important to note that these resources now extend beyond books and articles to recently filmed interviews and documentaries dedicated to these genres. Those entrusted with or who desire to teach this information must avail themselves of a broad spectrum of resources that will help church musicians, choristers, and congregations gain knowledge and understanding of the importance and significance of this music.

Another way of preserving these genres is by providing a structured curriculum or teaching program that provides historical, musical, and religious/spiritual information and significance of each. In my experience of more than forty years of presenting and performing these genres of music, I have discovered that many persons, particularly church attendees, are not aware of rich and diverse sacred music traditions of African ancestry that have emerged and evolved over centuries. It is particularly disheartening to hear persons under the age of forty remark that they have never heard of spirituals, or do not know that hymns constitute an entire genre of music or that there are more types of gospel music than what is currently popular. I wonder when I hear these statements why and how the teaching of these genres has been diminished within or omitted from church music programs altogether. Further, because general music education classes have been removed from most K–12 schools since the early 2000s, it is rare that today's school-age children receive any of this knowledge in a consistent, structured curriculum. I contend that, if knowledge and performance of these music genres are going to continue, they must be taught in a systematic manner.

TEACHING ANCESTRAL MUSIC IN THE CHURCH

How do we teach these genres in churches? I suggest three primary methods: 1) through ensemble singing, including children's, youth, and adult choirs; 2) through guest performances designed to bring attention to and highlight specific genres; and 3) through a structured music education curriculum taught throughout the year as a part of the overall Christian education program.

Ensemble Singing

Why is ensemble singing important in the life of the church? First, because it provides opportunities for people to offer their individual musical gifts and talents in group settings. Choirs and smaller singing ensembles can provide beautiful and meaningful selections which undergird the biblical or theological focus for a service. Second, because it provides opportunities for communal singing beyond congregational singing. While congregational singing is essential for worship, ensemble singing offers participants a more advanced level of music education, through consistent vocal training, exposure to a broader variety of music selections across multiple genres, and music history instruction. When songs are introduced in rehearsals, choral directors should offer some musical and historical background on the selections. This can help singers connect with music on a deeper level and realize the significance of the music and composers. Further, choral directors can use these teaching opportunities to talk about histories of specific genres of music that choirs are learning. This can lead to a fuller appreciation of and connection to music sung in worship, as well as histories of the peoples who created and performed this music over time.

Ensemble singing is also an effective tool for teaching music intergenerationally. Genres of music can be taught across multiple age levels, through appropriate song selection and vocal training. Histories of songs and genres can also be taught using techniques appropriate for specific age groups. Mass choirs comprised of all age groups can learn and sing certain selections together, providing opportunities for cross-generational encounters that can lead to sustained interest and participation in choral singing. Choral directors who desire to teach ensemble singing will need to know rudiments of vocal training for specific age groups, as well as teaching techniques to account for age-specific comprehension levels.

Guest Performances

Another way to teach music genres in the church is to invite guest singers and groups to present concerts, master classes, and workshops throughout the year. Church music departments might focus on one genre per quarter and have special presentations from that genre. Local college and university music departments are great resources for these events, and often the cost is nominal, particularly if students can use their participation for course or degree credit. When I chaired the church music department at a seminary, our music degree students often performed their capstone projects at area churches, and many times the churches used those performances as part of their quarterly music focus presentations. Another way to present these events without one church bearing the entire cost is to invite other churches or organizations to help sponsor the event. Community service organizations, public service entities, and even local businesses are often willing to sponsor events that are viewed as beneficial to the whole community, and music concerts, particularly those that include historical information as part of their presentations, are generally well received and attended by a generous cross section of community members. Neighborhood churches, churches grouped together by denominational affiliation, or other connections can partner to host music events together, dividing the cost while multiplying the number of attendees. This has the potential to expand the reach of these events, potentially expanding the dissemination of these rich and significant offerings.

Structured Music Education Curriculum

Ensuring the passage of historically and culturally significant information does not happen by accident. Even if churches are blessed with a plethora of musicians and choruses, that does not necessarily equate to structured pedagogy or systematic teaching. Choral directors often provide choir members with some level of vocal training and even some historical information on music selections. However, that does not provide the type of systematic instruction needed to produce musically astute, well-informed participants committed to preserving and performing historic music genres. A well-ordered, age-appropriate church music education curriculum led by knowledgeable, dedicated instructors has the potential to ensure sustainability of church music programs that incorporate a broad spectrum of musical offerings. It's important to note that a church music curriculum would not include the exact offerings of a school music curriculum; however, basic rudiments of vocal, instrumental, and choral music training along with introductory offerings in church music history should be standard instruction. As part of the church music history curriculum, classes in sacred music genres germane to African American worship should be offered throughout the year. Classes could be provided in modules that last anywhere from three to six weeks, depending on the depth of instruction and age level. Keeping the classes at a manageable length helps maintain interest and prevents instructor burnout. It would also allow churches to partner with local college music departments to provide students as instructors and receive course credit during semester classes.

THE IMPORTANCE OF PERFORMING HISTORIC GENRES IN WORSHIP

While guest performances can bring a lot of attention and attendance to music events, churches must not leave the responsibility for musical formation solely to professional musicians or academicians. Having music of diverse genres performed as part of weekly worship experiences is one of the best and most consistent methods of exposing people to and teaching them music history and its significance. What I contend is important is including the performance of a diverse cross section of music genres in every worship experience. While I am not suggesting including a particular genre in worship every Sunday, I am suggesting that historic genres of spirituals, hymns, and gospels should be performed every month with regularity. This helps congregations understand that these genres are not merely to be performed once a year as some tribute to the past, but that the past is and should always be present, and persons need to know the significance of these genres and how they can be used effectively in worship. Let's explore how this can be done throughout a particular month.

First, hymns can be employed almost every Sunday. Whatever the theme for a particular service might be there are generally multiple hymn titles based on that theme or the Scripture text which undergirds it. Singing congregational hymns regularly helps worshipers connect with the theme for a particular service while also helping lay out the theological understandings of a particular services theme. For example, in a worship service based on a biblical text about praising God, such as Ps 150, there are a plethora of hymns on praising God that can be sung, such as "Praise to the Lord, the Almighty," "To God Be the Glory, Great Things He Has Done," "Joyful, Joyful, We Adore Thee," and "Holy, Holy, Holy." Each of these hymns describes the wondrous and sovereign nature of God, the mighty acts of God in creation and in the lives of God's people, which is why we lift our voices communally in praise.

Further, singing congregational hymns, especially while using the hymnal, helps congregations with music reading as they can follow the melody on the music staff. Additionally, they learn hymn tunes that can be used interchangeably with other hymns of like meter. This can aid in congregations learning new hymns that are written in the same meter. For example, the hymn meter 8787 D can be sung to several hymn tunes, including "Converse," "Nettleton," "Bradbury," "Beach Spring," and "Beecher." Several well-known hymns, including "What a Friend We Have in Jesus," "Love Divine, All Loves Excelling," "Savior, Like a Shepherd Lead Us," and "Come Thou Fount of Every Blessing," are written in this meter. Each of these hymns can be sung to the previously mentioned hymn tunes. Singing hymns to different tunes can spark new interest in traditional hymns and allow worshipers to hear well-known hymns in a new way.

Spirituals can also be sung congregationally. Well-known spirituals such as "Every Time I Feel the Spirit," "Wade in the

Water," "Go Down, Moses," "Guide My Feet," and "He's Got the Whole World in His Hands" can provide a simple introduction to spirituals as a genre and help congregations, especially younger members, become acquainted with these historic songs and their significance to Black worshiping congregations. The singing of spirituals should not be limited to Black History Month but should be part and parcel of worship services and experiences throughout the Christian year. As congregations become more familiar with spirituals as a genre, additional titles can be added. Church musicians and choral directors can lead in teaching these songs to congregations and lead the singing of them in worship services.

Choirs should also be singing spirituals regularly. As worship planning teams meet to determine themes for individual services and to select music for these services, they should regularly select appropriate spirituals that coincide with the theme for the day. For example, if the theme is praising God, spirituals such as "Ain't Got Time to Die," "I'm Gonna Sing When the Spirit Says Sing," "Sunshine in My Soul," and "Great Day" would all be appropriate choral selections for that worship service. Singing spirituals well, especially when using choral arrangements, requires consistent practice. Churches who are committed to incorporating spirituals regularly must commit to employing proficient choral directors and musicians adept at teaching that particular genre. Choir members who are intent on learning how to sing spirituals must commit themselves to regular rehearsals.

Traditional and contemporary gospel music also deserve a regular place in worship. While many churches employ more current gospel songs, churches should not forget nor neglect to sing gospel standards, such as "Precious Lord," "How I Got Over," "Lord Keep Me Day by Day," "Peace, Be Still," "God Is," and "Revelation 19:1" ("Hallelujah, Salvation, and Glory"). Like other genres the use of gospel music in worship should coincide with the theme of the day. If the theme is praising God, gospel songs such as "Perfect Praise" ("How Excellent"), "Praise Him" ("Jesus, Blessed Savior"), "What a Mighty God We Serve," "I Will Call Upon the Lord," and "Let It Rise" are all appropriate gospel songs that focus on the praise and worship of God. Again, churches must be willing to invest in musicians who are capable of teaching and playing gospel songs, both traditional and contemporary.

INCLUDING MUSIC GENRES IN CHURCHES THROUGHOUT THE YEAR

What are some practical methods for keeping these genres incorporated into worship services throughout the year? Four in particular that I suggest would be quite effective are: 1) singing songs from one particular genre in multiple worship services each quarter of the calendar year; 2) singing songs from one particular genre in multiple worship services within a liturgical season of the Christian year; 3) inviting guest musicians who specialize in a particular genre to participate in selected worship services; and 4) inserting brief presentations about a particular genre in worship services bimonthly or once a quarter. We will examine each of these ideas briefly.

Singing Songs of a Particular Genre

To provide systematic instruction on a particular genre of music, there must be a sustained effort to keep the focus on that genre. Intentionally including songs of a certain music genre in worship services throughout each quarter of the calendar year allows congregations to become imbued with the characteristics of that music. This is not to suggest that every song in a worship service would be of one genre, but to sing at least one song of a genre in at least two worship services a month would help singers and worshipers connect with the sound and quality of the music of that genre. Moreover, it would give music departments an opportunity to learn and present the varying types of songs in a particular genre. For example, most music historians assert that there are three types of spirituals: 1) slow, sustained melodies such as found in songs like "Deep River"; 2) syncopated, segmented melodies, such as "Little

David, Play on Your Harp"; and 3) call-and-response songs, such as "Certainly, Lord." Focusing on one genre per quarter would give choirs an opportunity to learn these varied types of spirituals and present them in multiple services, providing congregations opportunities to hear and learn the unique aspects of each type.

Performing Genres Within Liturgical Seasons

A similar method for keeping a particular genre at the musical forefront of worship is to sing songs from one genre within a liturgical season of the Christian year. In most liturgical seasons, there are at least four Sundays, if not six or more. Music departments could present congregational and choral music within a genre in each of these worship services. Let's explore how this could be accomplished in the season of Lent. I have provided the Lenten lectionary texts of each Sunday of the Year C cycle in figure 6.1. Within each block there are titles[1] listed in each genre (hymn, spiritual, traditional gospel, and contemporary gospel)[2] that align with one or more of the Scripture texts. During the Lenten season, music departments would program at least one of the songs in the chosen genre (not across genres) into the weekly worship service. Most of the songs listed can be sung congregationally, as well as chorally, which would allow everyone to participate, rather than limit participation to a few select singers.

---

1. For the purposes of this table, hymns are attributed to the original lyricist, while traditional and contemporary gospels are identified by recording artists who popularized the song, followed by the name of the composer(s).

2. For the purposes of this table, traditional gospel is defined as gospel songs recorded before the year 1990; contemporary gospel is songs recorded after 1990.

Preserving the Gift of African-Descended Sacred Music

Figure 6.1

Lent Year C	First reading	Psalm	Second reading	Gospel
ABBREVIATIONS KEY: H: Hymn LH: Lined/Metered Hymn S: Spiritual TG: Traditional Gospel CG: Contemporary Gospel				
Ash Wednesday H/S: "Lord, I Want to Be a Christian" (Trad.) S: "I Want Jesus to Walk with Me" TG: "Give Me a Clean Heart" (James Cleveland/Margaret Douroux) CG: "Change Me, O God" (solo) (Tamela Mann/Tamela Mann and Thomas Clay)	Joel 2:1–2, 12–17 or Isa 58:1–12	Ps 51:1–17	2 Cor 5:20b–6:10	Matt 6:1–6, 16–21
First Sunday in Lent H: "Lord, Who Throughout These Forty Days" (Claudia Hernaman) S: "Jesus Walked This Lonesome Valley" S/TG: "Jesus Is a Rock in a Weary Land" CG: "Safety" (Lecresia Campbell/Oscar Williams)	Deut 26:1–11	Ps 91:1–2, 9–16	Rom 10:8b–13	Luke 4:1–13
Second Sunday in Lent H: "I Am Thine, O Lord" (Fanny Crosby) S: "City Called Heaven" TG: "The Lord Is My Light and My Salvation" (James Cleveland/Lillian Bouknight) CG: "Everlasting God" (William Murphy)	Gen 15:1–12, 17–18	Ps 27	Phil 3:17–4:1	Luke 13:31–35 or Luke 9:28–36 (37–43a)

Lent Year C	First reading	Psalm	Second reading	Gospel
Third Sunday in Lent LH: "Guide Me, O Thou Great Jehovah" (William Williams) S: "Seek the Lord" TG: "Search Me, Lord" (Mahalia Jackson/Thomas Dorsey) CG: "You're the Lifter of My Head" (Ricky Dillard/Derrick Hall)	Isa 55:1–9	Ps 63:1–8	1 Cor 10:1–13	Luke 13:1–9
Fourth Sunday in Lent H: "Great Is Thy Faithfulness" (Thomas Chisholm) S: "I Believe I'll Go Back Home" (solo) S: "King Jesus Is A-Listenin'" TG: "Trouble in My Way" (Albertina Walker/Don Robey and Ira Tucker Jr.) CG: "You Know My Name" (Tasha Cobbs Leonard/Tasha Cobbs Leonard and Brenton Gifford Brown)	Josh 5:9–12	Ps 32	2 Cor 5:16–21	Luke 15:1–3, 11b–32
Fifth Sunday in Lent H: "Higher Ground" (Johnson Oatman Jr.) S: "Little Innocent Lamb" TG: "Move On Up a Little Higher" (solo) (Mahalia Jackson/W. Herbert Brewster) CG: "When Sunday Comes" (Daryl Coley feat. Donald Lawrence and the Tri-City Singers/Donald Lawrence) CG: "Alabaster Box" (solo) (CeCe Winans/Janice Sjostran) CG: "For Every Mountain" (Kurt Carr)	Isa 43:16–21	Ps 126	Phil 3:4b–14	John 12:1–8

Lent Year C	First reading	Psalm	Second reading	Gospel
Sixth Sunday in Lent Liturgy of the Palms H: "Hosanna, Loud Hosannas" (Jeanette Threlfall) S: "Ride On, King Jesus" TG: "Ride On, King Jesus/In That Great Getting Up Morning" (Trad.) CG: "Lord, You Are Good" (Israel Houghton)		Ps 118:1–2, 19–29		Luke 19:28–40
Sixth Sunday in Lent Liturgy of the Passion H: "What Wondrous Love Is This" (Folk hymn) S: "He Never Said a Mumblin' Word" (solo) S: "I've Been 'Buked and I've Been Scorned" TG: "I Find No Fault in God" (The Caravans feat. Shirley Caesar/Ernest Franklin) CG: "Safe from Harm" (solo) (BeBe Winans/Linda Thompson) CG: "Just for Me" (Donnie McClurkin)	Isa 50:4–9a	Ps 31:9–16	Phil 2:5–11	Luke 22:14–23:56 or Luke 23:1–49

Inviting Guest Musicians Throughout the Year

Inviting guest musicians as a part of focusing on a particular music genre can be extremely effective, if planned and executed intentionally. Bringing in soloists or ensembles who perform certain genres with professionalism and excitement can spark additional interest in the music being presented. If churches decide to include outside participants, prior legwork is necessary to ensure continuity with the stated foci and appropriateness within the context of the worship service in which they will participate. Those who are planning the service will need to research singers and/or groups and contact them about performing. When making contact, questions regarding repertoire, instrumentation, and staging are crucial to determining which Sundays would be best for them to appear. It would be most helpful for the church to have a suggested song list prepared before contacting outside performers, as one of the goals of the worship service is for the music to undergird the day's message or theme. However, if the soloist or group does not have a particular song in its repertoire, it may still be possible for them to perform, if the music staff includes in its introduction of the group an explanation of why the singers are presenting the chosen selections.

Besides singing selections, churches can focus attention on a particular genre by setting aside time within the worship service to offer presentations that define, describe, and provide history of said genres. Ideally, this would be presented through the church's music education class participants. A brief presentation of no more than five or six minutes can pique interest in a subject, and if done creatively can elicit spirited responses from congregants. These presentations can be done several times a quarter, or once or twice during a liturgical season. The keys to making them meaningful are consistency, intentionality, and excellence.

Presenting Information About Genres in Worship

In addition to making sure these genres are sung regularly in worship, there must be intentional methods employed to teach their respective histories. It is not enough to teach congregations, choirs, or praise teams to sing these songs; as previously discussed, a sound music curriculum must be put in place to provide historical and musical insight into each genre. One method would be to introduce information about these genres in actual worship services. Designated persons could take five minutes over a given number of Sundays to share the history and significance of a particular genre and note its incorporation into that specific worship service or recent worship services. This helps congregations learn, not only cognitively, but also experientially, by connecting the historical information about the genre with its musical performance.

DEALING WITH PUSHBACK

What if congregational members do not see the benefits of providing systematic music instruction in churches? What if some do not appreciate focusing on historic genres in worship? Before you comment that no one could argue against including hymns, spirituals, and gospel music into worship service, let me assure you I have experienced pushback against all of these throughout my almost fifty-year church music career. I have had church and choir members argue against singing spirituals because they considered them "slave music." I've had people rail against including contemporary gospel music because it was "too secular." Likewise, some congregations push back against certain types of hymns, especially unfamiliar tunes, and I've heard arguments against both original and contemporary hymn lyrics. Additionally, churches have not wanted to spend the money to provide music training/courses throughout the year or to bring in professional singers or groups. Why do these critiques exist and what can be done to address them?

First, there is no way to please everyone in any given situation, and any attempt to do so is futile. Second, sometimes people offer criticisms of certain initiatives because they are unaware of the benefits that can be gained. If someone has not been taught the value of appreciating various types of music, chances are they are not going to have an open mind when it comes to experiencing music they do not care for. Third, unfortunately, people have been taught, either by precept or example, that certain music has no worth or benefit because of its origins or if it shines a light on negative histories or perceptions. That is certainly the case with spirituals, which were born out of the brutality and horrors of enslavement. Some brief (and incorrect) histories about spirituals, as a genre, would have people believe that they were the minstrel songs that enslaved persons sang for the benefit of slaveholders.

If that is the only information an individual ever learned about spirituals, and/or the individual's knowledge about the antebellum period caused them to only have a negative perception about African and African-descended ancestry and artistry, that person would not receive the spirituals as one of the original American art forms, worthy of remembrance and continued performance.

Addressing these critiques and perceptions requires forethought, openness, and patience. Reacting to them with an elitist air as though critics are uneducated or uncouth because they think or feel differently is a sure way to create unnecessary conflict and prevent any musical horizon broadening that might be accomplished. Rather, the use of subtle approaches that involve offering fuller and more accurate historical landscapes of these genres can help shift perceptions and open doors to better reception of the music. Being prepared to counter criticisms and false historical data is the responsibility of those who desire to teach the worth and wealth of these genres. Therefore, choral directors, church musicians, and even pastoral staff must be prepared to address any pushback against the presentation of the music being offered for instruction. This can be accomplished in rehearsals, in workshops, and in worship services, if presenters have done their research fully and are prepared to present in a way that everyone can receive what is being offered.

7

Afrofuturist and Ancestral Worship Connections

I've heard of a city called Heaven
I'm trying to make it my home.
—Traditional Spiritual

THE CONCEPT OF FUTURING

WE HAVE EXAMINED ANCESTRAL sacred music genres and how churches might continue to keep them alive in worship. Now, let us turn our attention to Afrofuturism: how, as a conceptual framework, it can help congregations "future" their worship practices and experiences, and how ancestral music helps make those Afrofuturist connections. What does "futuring" mean? The word "future" is defined as "the time or a period of time following the moment of speaking or writing; time regarded as still to come."[1] "Futuring" is defined as "the practice of envisioning and planning

1. Lexicon of Design Research, "Futuring."

for potential futures, often through a systematic process that includes analysis, exploration, and forecasting."[2] According to the Lexicon of Design Research:

> The term "futuring" has its roots in the post-World War II era. Scientists, politicians, and academics began to consider ways of anticipating the future, this led, among other things, to the founding of the World Future Society in the mid-1960s. The concept of "futuring" has been, and still is, widely used in innovation research.[3]

Really Good Innovation provides this description of "futuring":

> Futuring is a critical tool in innovation management. It is an approach to designing future scenarios based on current trends, opportunities, and challenges. By leveraging data-driven insights about what could happen in the future, "futuring" helps organizations anticipate change and shape their strategies accordingly. It can be used to inform decision making across multiple areas such as product development, customer experience design, marketing strategies, resource allocation, and organizational culture.[4]

A sociological understanding of "futuring" is described in the *European Journal of Social Theory* as "the identification, creation and dissemination of images of the future shaping the possibility space action, thus enacting relationships between past, present and future."[5]

Each of these definitions contains essential components for comprehending the varied meanings and significance of "futuring" as a concept. From the fields of innovation and design research, we see the importance of envisioning and planning, using a systematic approach, to posit future scenarios. This systematic approach requires real-time analyses of current trends, opportunities, and challenges. The outcomes of such analyses have the

2. Lucas, "20/20 Foresight," para. 7.
3. Lexicon of Design Research, "Futuring," para. 1.
4. Really Good Innovation, "Futuring," para. 1.
5. Oomen et al., "Techniques of Futuring," 257.

potential to impact systems across a wide range of areas. Looking at "futuring" through a sociological lens can help us determine the impacts of "futuring" on human behavior, individually and across communities.

Though "futuring" might have had its beginnings in science and academics, the techniques and tools of this radical concept have tremendous implications for the church. First, the steady decline of membership and attendance across denominations and faith communities of almost every designation and description over the past thirty years calls for an examination of methods and practices designed to retain and attract members. Second, addressing this decline requires major shifts in these methods and practices. This is where "futuring" can potentially have a definite positive impact. By using systematic and strategic analyses of current data around trends, opportunities, and challenges, and exploring possibilities through visioning and forecasting, churches can work to envision what their futures might hold. Before we examine the importance of "futuring" churches, let us look at where the church is currently, particularly in the areas of societal perception and worship attendance.

THE CURRENT STATE OF WORSHIP ATTENDANCE

The decline of membership in mainline Christian churches has been occurring for the last several decades, according to statistics from the Pew Research Center.[6] Aaron Earls, editor of the Facts and Trends website, authored two articles that speak specifically to this decline, one written in 2016 and the other seven years later. Both outline several reasons why millennials and Gen Z-ers are not attending worship. We'll examine several of these reasons below.

---

6. G. Smith et al., "In U.S., Decline of Christianity."

You aren't online.

According to "A Brief History of the Internet,"[7] the internet officially began on January 1, 1983. The generation known as millennials and successive generations, therefore, do not know a time before the internet. Most grew up with some access to computers and social networking sites, however limited, earning the descriptor "digital natives." One result of this access is an expectation that businesses, organizations, and even churches have a current digital footprint. Many people forty and younger find churches to attend by searching and researching area churches online Monday through Saturday rather than making "cold calls" on a Sunday morning. If churches do not have current websites, especially ones that are eye catching, more than likely, they will not attract these age groups.

You are too inward focused.

While many individuals classify themselves as "spiritual" rather than "religious," often they still have a desire to connect with community, particularly with the goal of helping those in need. According to Earls, though "millennials have a reputation of being self-absorbed, they passionately support causes that inspire them."[8] If they attempt to become part of a church and find that the bulk of its time and resources are spent on those inside the four walls of the sanctuary, they will find somewhere else to attend.

You aren't trustworthy.

I have often heard people remark that "church people" are the most judgmental, gossipy, and envious people they've ever encountered. If a church gains the reputation of being a place where people cannot feel safe being themselves, it will not garner new members and will steadily lose the younger members it has. Most young people

---

7 Board of Regents, "Brief History," 2.
8. Earls, "Six Reasons," para. 7.

are not interested in spending their free time in places where they do not feel affirmed or with people they feel they cannot trust with their truth.

You aren't diverse.

While many churches are comfortable with homogeneity and see no reason to make efforts to broaden their attendance/attraction base, many Gen Y and Z members want to be part of faith communities that "draw the circle wide." Their worlds are comprised of varying activities that include individuals from a wide array of demographic backgrounds, and they want to see that reflected in the places they worship and fellowship.

You are too institutional.

What is often meant by "too institutional" is a group or organization that places business interests above people's needs. If the "bottom line" for a church is profits or purely numbers of people attending, and not the spiritual growth or maturity of those attending, people are turned off, particularly those who see themselves as "spiritual," but not necessarily religious. Millennials typically avoid institutions, especially ones that are not invested in the betterment of their people.

You don't offer real community.

Churches that are not invested or involved in the communities in which they reside will not attract new constituencies. This can be a thorny issue for historic churches that have been sitting on certain properties for decades or centuries. However, if a church no longer addresses that community's needs or if the surrounding communities have shifted to significantly impact the identity of the neighborhood, the church must adapt to the changes, so it can continue its work in those communities. Further, members, especially younger members, want opportunities to connect with each other outside of the worship experience, through small group activities that focus on fellowship.

You don't have anyone under forty in visible leadership.

Often, church leaders decry the lack of youth and young adults in worship, affirm the need for young people to pass the baton to, and openly state that they are the church of tomorrow. However, how many churches have individuals under the age of forty in visible leadership positions? How many Sundays a month do youth and young adults lead in worship, how many boards and auxiliaries are headed by youth and young adults, and how often are youth and young adults consulted about their ideas for evangelism, discipleship, worship, or spiritual formation? If young people attend a church and don't see young people in leadership on a consistent basis, more than likely they are not going to commit to membership there.

You don't have a current website or social media presence.

It is simply amazing the number of church websites I visit in a week that have outdated information on their websites, don't have relevant information about the church on the home page (address, service times, names of leadership, etc.), or have links to pages that have no information listed. Very few people currently use hardcopy directories to locate goods and services; most find what they are looking for through an internet browser search. And while churches may be listed online under "Churches near me," if the church does not have a current and active website, most people will not seek it out to attend.

Likewise, if churches do not have a social media footprint, it will be difficult to draw new people who know nothing about the church. A website gives an online visitor the ability to find out basic information about the church and its ministries. However, an active social media presence gives the church the ability to interact with virtual visitors. Posts about weekly activities, live streams of worship, and photos of ministry efforts give virtual visitors a chance to comment or inquire about what the church is doing currently in communities.

To have attractive websites and social media pages, churches need to invest in good web designers and administrators. That does not necessarily mean spending a lot of money; there may be people in the church presently, including youth and young adults, who can produce and monitor an active website and social media page. It just takes some effort to find and work with them to generate an appealing web presence.

SEVEN YEARS AGO VS. TODAY

In his more recent article, Earls discovered that one of the biggest impacts on church membership and attendance today is the COVID-19 pandemic.[9] In March 2020, the world came to a screeching halt as COVID-19 spread its tentacles across the globe. Almost seven million people have died as a result of the pandemic, with millions more impacted in every facet of everyday life. One of the institutions most affected by the outbreak was the church. Statistics from the Pew Research Group report that of those adults attending in-person religious services less often than before the pandemic, 51 percent state that worry about COVID-19 is a reason. When asked about watching religious services online, 50 percent of respondents say it's safer than attending in person.

Other reasons associated with the pandemic that also account for the decline in church attendance include comfort (people have simply become comfortable watching services online), challenges, including physical challenges that make attending difficult, and changes (people discovered other ways to pursue their spiritual interests and found they did not miss church).

People found that they did not miss church.

9. Earls, "Four Reasons."

THE NEED FOR MEANINGFUL WORSHIP

What an indictment! What do I mean? How tragic is it that those who stopped attending because they did not miss it did not have any pertinent reasons to return. Whatever was going on in worship and other ministries was not significant enough to be considered necessary for their well-being. Of course, some people did return, but many more did not, and part of the reason was because they did not see the need. Why did they not see the need to return? I am sure there are several reasons, but one I have heard repeatedly from those who have not gone back (and are not even watching virtually) is that worship services, in particular, hold no real meaning for them. What does that mean? People are seeking meaning in today's world, in their relationships, in their vocations and careers, and in their spiritual practices. Many are not willing to continue attending churches out of tradition, obligation, or habit. People want their lives to matter, and they want what they do with their lives to matter, at work, at play, and in communion with the Divine. It is no longer sufficient for them to sit in a one- or two-hour-long worship service singing hymns and reciting creeds they don't understand or agree with, listening to sermons and prayers that don't answer their deep questions, and being sent out of the doors without truly understanding their place and purpose in this life.

For many people in today's world, worship must connect them with their divinely ordained purposes in ways they can comprehend. Elements of worship including Scripture, song, prayer, and ritual must combine to create spiritually meaningful experiences that can be applied practically in daily life. Further, they want to be participants in the worship experience and not merely spectators. In too many churches, attendees spend a great deal of time passively watching worship—listening to choral selections, listening to clergy speaking, watching action in front of them rather than participating actively in singing, reading, reciting, and responding. Nothing is wrong with active listening; however, congregations should have a participatory role in worship in which they are doing the action that is occurring. This is the true meaning of liturgy, from the Greek word *leitourgia*, which means "work of the people." Worship experiences should reflect and include the very people who are present in the experience. This is how true spiritual connection and growth occurs, through participation in meaningful experiences that have the power to transform.

Meaningful worship transforms. It transforms individuals, who then transform communities, who have the power to transform the world. One reason why communities in neighborhoods with dozens of churches on every corner do not become transformed is because many churches are insulated from the communities they inhabit. The churches are not concerned with what is going on outside the four walls of the edifice; they are preoccupied only with the members inside. They are not aware or interested in the demographics or statistics that impact these communities; they are content every week to drive in for service and then right back out again. How meaningful could the weekly worship experience be if it is not spurring members to become a vital part of their community?

Perhaps the problem is that worship experiences in these churches are not meaningful. Perhaps they have become mundane and stale, ritualistic and repetitive, and attendees are not inspired. Perhaps it is because the worship is not authentic to its current congregation. Just because certain worship styles and music genres were part and parcel of a church's worship experience years ago does not mean these same styles and genres are still serving the church well today. Further, orders of worship that have remained the same over years (even decades) may need to be revisited to determine if changes are warranted to help current congregants connect more readily.

Moreover, we need to examine how we determine what makes worship meaningful. It is not just about whether I "liked" or "enjoyed" a worship service, but did it produce any change within me which then inspired me to help transform my church and community? Part of the way we determine what makes worship meaningful is by examining the lenses through which we view worship. All of us have certain lenses through which we ascribe meaning, and this includes the churches we attend. These include the following:

- Christian—How do we determine what is Christian in our worshiping context? What makes the worship in our churches Christian? Where do we point people when they ask about how we mean "Christianity" in our church's context?

- Denominational—How do we worship in our denomination? Is our worship order/liturgy identical to another church's order/liturgy in our denomination? If it is not, why not? Did we change it to better serve the people in our particular church's context?

- Liturgical—How do we worship in our church? Why did our church arise as an independent congregation? How does that impact our worship? How did our church's worship order/liturgy develop? Has it changed since the church's inception? If so, was it to better serve the people in our church's context?

- Experiential—How do we experience worship? Do we connect primarily with our intellect? Emotion? Sensory awareness? Meditative or contemplative approaches? What acts of worship draw us in more than others? How do we remember our worship experiences? How do we connect them with the other facets of our lives?

- Liberative—How does our worship help set us free? How does it help us embody the *imago Dei* (the image of God) as disciples who go out to share the good news of the gospel of Jesus?

THE FUTURE OF
AFRICAN AMERICAN WORSHIP

If meaningful worship that has the power to transform individuals and communities is what the church is seeking to produce, what are the strategies, tools, and resources it needs to accomplish that? I would contend that before churches determine strategies or look for tools or resources, they need to seek a vision for themselves that looks beyond where they are presently, a vision that futures them and the congregations that comprise them. What does it mean to "future" oneself or one's community? As we stated previously, "futuring" means using a systematic approach to posit future scenarios, using visioning and planning to analyze current trends, opportunities, and challenges to surmise where an entity or organization is, in efforts to "see" what and where the organization can be in the future. If the Christian church, particularly the African American/Black church hopes to "see" itself in the future, it must do the work now of "futuring" itself. What systematic process would be helpful for African American faith communities to use to "future" themselves? I would recommend employing an Afrofuturist ideology and methodology for this work.

WHAT IS AFROFUTURISM?

Ytasha Womack, Afrofuturist author and scholar, tells us that Afrofuturism is "an intersection of imagination, technology, the future, and liberation; both an artistic aesthetic and a framework for critical theory."[10] The term "Afrofuturist" was coined by Mark Dery in 1994 to describe new ways Black college students and artists were analyzing art and sociology through technological and cultural lenses. What were some of the reasons for these new analyses? According to Womack:

> Afrofuturists sought to unearth the missing history of people of African descent and their roles in science, technology, and science fiction. They also aimed to reintegrate people of color into the discussion of cyberculture, modern science, technology, and sci-fi pop culture. . . . They hoped to facilitate equal access to progressive technologies, in an effort to diminish the race-based power imbalance—and hopefully color-based limitations—for good.[11]

10. Womack, *Afrofuturism*, 21.
11. Womack, *Afrofuturism*, 21–22.

Afrofuturism seeks to counter narratives that relegate African and African-descended cultures and traditions to second-class status, particularly stereotypical notions about Africans and their descendants in the diaspora, especially those that arose during and after the antebellum period in America. Further, Afrofuturism seeks to counter negative perspectives of nihilism and Afro-pessimism, neither of which provides hope for the future of Africans and their descendants. Moreover, and to the point of why I am advocating Afrofuturism as a framework for "futuring" worship, Afrofuturism posits and affirms the presence and perpetuation of African peoples in the future. That outlook is critical if the Black church as a foundational institution and its various faith communities are going to envision a thriving way forward.

How does Afrofuturism help with this vision? Womack states that Afrofuturism "values the power of creativity and imagination to reinvigorate culture and transcend social limitations. The resilience of the human spirit lies in our ability to imagine."[12] Ingrid LaFleur states, "I generally define Afrofuturism as a way of imagining possible futures through a black cultural lens. I see Afrofuturism as a way to encourage experimentation, reimagine identities, and activate liberation."[13] Why is imagination so essential to the future of Black worshiping communities? I contend that imagination offers four main avenues that move worship forward. Imagination:

- Spurs creativity—Worship that lacks imagination lacks creativity. One of the main critiques of today's worship is that it is staid and routine, rituals have become mundane and perfunctory, orders of service are predictable and stale, the worshiper experiences very little inspiration and thus very little, if any, transformation. The use of imagination in planning, implementing, and participating in worship opens new creative possibilities in these experiences that can potentially inspire and transform individuals and communities. Worship

12. Womack, *Afrofuturism*, 27.
13. LaFleur, "Visual Aesthetics," 01:10–01:26.

becomes an opportunity to use creativity intentionally to reform, reshape, and revise worship practices to better engage worshipers in what can become much more meaningful experiences.

- Helps us envision and interpret texts—Imagination is an essential tool in exegeting, or interpreting, biblical (and other) texts. Reading any text requires one to use imagination to "see" what the author means or point to in a narrative. Reading texts that are millennia of years old certainly requires the ability to envision in the mind's eye what the authors might be saying and meaning, first, to the original community to whom the narrative was written, and then, to the contemporary reader or hearer. The ability to comprehend the meanings of other languages (even when translated), metaphors, allegories, tropes, parables, analogies, signs, and symbols requires imagination to broaden the scope

- Provides avenues for inclusion and diversity—A desire to include all persons in their full embodiment and identities in ways that honor, respect, and affirm them as children of God requires imaginations that see beyond false or contrived boundaries. Imagination helps worship planners and practitioners envision and create worship services that welcome, include, and engage all worshipers in the fullness of their authentic personhoods.

- Acts as a tool of resistance, along with improvisation and adaptability—Imagination works to counter oppression, because it empowers the user to see beyond what is, to what could be. Though systems of injustice may seem unconquerable, imagination helps people, especially people of faith, to envision dismantling and discarding these systems, while helping them construct life-giving realities.

Black peoples have always had to use imagination, improvisation, and adaptability to survive and thrive in the world. We have never had the luxury of having our humanity fully affirmed or accepted, nor has Blackness ever been centered or believed to be beautiful, good, or worthy of affirmation. Across the globe, even on the continent, colonization has wreaked havoc on the self-worth and perception of peoples of African descent. Blackness has been demonized, denigrated, and made the dividing line between life and death. Marginalization of Black peoples historically has included murder, enslavement, and segregation, in efforts to remove them from the face of the earth. Therefore, Black peoples have had to find multiplicities of ways to survive and thrive across time and space. Our ability to imagine, improvise, and adapt has kept and sustained us over millennia while also providing avenues for joy, respite, and growth.

Scholar Reynaldo Anderson reminds us that techniques of these tools that show up in our cultural and spiritual lexicons include "signifying, call-and-response, narrative sequencing, tonal semantics, technological rhetoric, agitation, Africana womanist or black feminist epistemologies, queer studies, and visual rhetoric."[14] We will say more about these later, but what is important to note is that Black peoples created and have always used these techniques to help us navigate a world that rarely seemed to fully include us. This means Afrofuturism as a conceptual framework has always been with us; we have always used technology, whether scientific, organic, or spiritual, to "future" ourselves.

Historically, our worship has been underscored by the same tenets and techniques of Afrofuturism: "imagination, hope, and expectation for transformative change."[15] What has been the history of Black worship, particularly in America? Despite the circumstances in which enslaved Africans found themselves in the diaspora, they still believed in the power and efficacy of their gods and held enough experiential memory of rites and rituals to summon their presence and assistance. Through successive generations, those who were still arriving from African countries would have shared their religious practices, as best they could, in hopes that their ritual remembrances and honoring of their gods would produce the end of their suffering. Even after the so-called

---

14. Anderson, "Critical Afrofuturism," 175.
15. Womack, *Afrofuturism*, 43.

Afrofuturist and Ancestral Worship Connections

death of the African gods,[16] *AfricansinAmerica* continued to infuse their worship with practices steeped in African traditions and retentions.

Though many of them accepted Christianity (sometimes begrudgingly), slaveholders would have been surprised to know that *AfricansinAmerica* conflated this Christian god with the identities and attributes of African gods, particularly the "High God," and that Jesus and the Holy Spirit were viewed as intermediaries, tasked with serving as the imminent and very real presence of the "High God" and doing God's work in the world. Further, many enslaved persons developed and celebrated the existence of an entire mediating system of saints, known to them as African and African-descended ancestors. The religious practices in which they engaged were imbued with Africanisms that survived across continents and centuries—Africanisms that lived and live within African and African-descended rituals and liturgical practices in North America. The legacy of African ritual as a practice was evinced in the ways that enslaved Africans and their descendants developed worship practices during the antebellum period. The development of brush arbor or "hush" arbor worship, which became identified as the *invisible institution*, grew out of the enslaved Africans' insistence on worshiping in ways that re-membered African rites and rituals.

Inherent in and infused throughout these worship events were signs, symbols, and testimonies of God-consciousness—an acknowledgment and internalization of sacred cosmos, expressions of kinship vertically and horizontally, spirit possession, melodic and rhythmic aspects of music, and prayer. The music, preacher, and frenzy that Du Bois references and that slave narratives testify to experiencing provide a consistent picture of the survival and preservation of African retentions in worship. These retentions exemplify the presence and practice of spiritual technologies such as those previously mentioned, including call-and-response, improvisation, technological rhetoric, agitation, and womanist/liberationist epistemologies, as well as the use of

---

16. See Raboteau, *Slave Religion*, 43–94.

folklore in tales that included both affirmation and signifying as rhetorical devices. These characteristics also testify to the presence and power of African heritages, including the importance of private, divine space where persons were free to worship, freedom of the Spirit to indwell those gathered and permeate the space with divine, transformative power, communal affinity and care for one another, and preaching that was both inspiring and sensitive to the fragile, fledgling community.

HISTORICAL WORSHIP THEMES

The four main themes of Black worship during (and beyond) the antebellum period were survival, resistance, deliverance and liberation, and affirmation and joy. We will examine each of these themes below.

Survival

The *invisible institution* arose out of the need for *AfricansinAmerica* to experience a safe, divine space that signified freedom amid oppression. Though the ability to worship freely meant sacrificing one's time and taking serious risks to personal well-being, *AfricansinAmerica* were determined to engage space and place that affirmed their humanity and connections with the Creator and each other.

Resistance

Enslaved persons who worshiped in slaveholder churches could not reveal their true feelings about what was being preached, taught, or sung, and often had to produce evidence that they understood and agreed with the catechism being taught. But in the worship of the *invisible institution*, they were able to shed these masks and worship authentically, calling on the names of their gods, singing ancestral-inspired songs, and engaging in practices that allowed them direct communion with the Holy. These acts of resistance spoke to and affirmed their humanity, giving them the strength to continue pressing on in the face of unrelenting inhumanity.

Deliverance and Liberation

These two concepts, though slightly different in definition, performed/behaved almost identically in Black antebellum worship. The spiritual experience of "getting religion" or being converted resulted in the transformation of hearts, souls, and minds of enslaved persons, if not their bodies. There was an empowerment that occurred through the worship experience, particularly the event of being indwelt by the Spirit. Not only were individuals assured of their humanity in these moments, but they felt a kind of freedom from the daily persecutions they endured, which remained with them after the initial event ended. Brush arbor worship experiences also empowered enslaved persons to participate in freedom movements. Slave revolts, uprisings, and insurrections often came on the heels of ecstatic worship services where persons received prophetic visions, particularly after reading or hearing certain biblical passages preached, that demanded armed response to the institution of slavery.

Affirmation and Joy

AfricansinAmerica found in the worship experience, among other events, an opportunity to exult, to celebrate, to rejoice, not only in the acts of prayer, singing, preaching, and shouting, not only in conversion or "getting religion," but in the affirmation of their humanity within community. Those who had experienced the indwelling of the Holy Spirit, and who had been converted or simply continued to believe in the gods of their ancestors, while making room for the god of the Israelites and Mary's little *boy-chile*, Jesus, navigated life by a new star—that of incandescent hope, which glowed deep inside.

AfricansinAmerica in the antebellum period were generally not interested in or affected by white mores or values, especially since these mores and values rang hollow and were hypocritical in the light of the brutal treatment suffered at their hands. Moreover, the African inheritance of communal existence and belief in the constant abiding presence of the Holy provided a sense of authenticity required for living as a true community member. In the Black antebellum aesthetic, this came forth in the full appreciation of all manner of creative expressions, "holy and profane, good and evil, the beautiful and dreadful."[17] Resisting and/or rejecting performative *respectability politics* of white church worship, *AfricansinAmerica* gave themselves up "with shouts of joy and 'singing feet' to this wholeness of being, to the ecstatic celebration of one's creaturehood."[18]

After emancipation, these organic, scientific, and spiritual technologies continued to "future" Black worshiping spaces in the developments of praise/pray's houses, independent congregations, and Black denominations. While some spaces included religious traditions adapted from white congregations and denominational traditions, most retained African and African-descended practices and elements of worship, including prayers, Black music and preaching, shouting, and fellowshiping during and after services. We also can see these technologies present in the ways African-descended worshiping communities practiced resistance in the face of continued oppression and injustice. Black denominations such as the African Methodist Episcopal Church, the African Methodist Episcopal Zion Church, the Christian Methodist Episcopal Church, the National Baptist Convention of America, the National Baptist Convention, USA, the Church of God in Christ, and independent Pentecostal, Holiness, Apostolic, and Sanctified churches arose after emancipation and during Reconstruction to provide African-descended persons, in particular, a haven to worship freely, as their ancestors did in the *invisible institution*. Further, many of these communities participated in abolitionist

---

17. Wilmore, *Black Religion*, 34.
18. Wilmore, *Black Religion*, 34.

organizations and activities and advocated for the social, economic, political, and self-determining well-being of *all* people, but most explicitly, Black people.

AN ESSENTIAL AFROFUTURIST LENS

> Afrofuturistic consciousness yields a vision of Blackness that, while it may respond to white supremacy, is not bound by whiteness.[19]

Melva Costen asserts that Black worship in North America evolved from four main strands: traditional African primal worldviews; Judeo-Christian religion; African American folk religion, and Western/Euro-American Christianity. Further, she posits that African American Christians share several common aspects of worship regardless of denomination. They are: 1) gathering to offer thanks and praise to God in and through Jesus Christ, and to be spiritually fed by the word of God; 2) a common historical taproot, extending deep into the African soil; and 3) our history of struggle for survival as African people in America.[20] Claiming that Africans did not know God when they arrived on North American shores is patently false. John Mbiti notes in his groundbreaking research of African peoples, "In all these societies, without a single exception, people have a notion of God."[21] Africans brought their cosmological and theological views to American shores and, despite barriers of communication, distrust, and fear, were able to create sacred space for themselves and their descendants to worship in ways that were authentic and meaningful.

Even with these spaces, African-descended people were still surrounded and beset by anti-Black theologies and ideologies, in the slaveholders' churches and by plantation preachers endowed with religious authority from slaveholders to hold sanctioned services for enslaved individuals. In these churches and their services

---

19. Sneed, *Dreamer and the Dream*, 1.
20. Costen, *African American Christian Worship*, 1–10.
21. Mbiti, *African Religions and Philosophy*, 29.

ran a constant current of anti-Blackness that made itself visible in Puritan and Anglican theological tenets such as visible sainthood, divine superiority, hereditary heathenism, and paternalism. All of these were based in the belief that Blackness was evil, or at the very least, inferior to whiteness, and required evangelization to become less evil/heathen/savage by becoming as "pure" (read: white) as possible. No amount of evangelism, however, could completely overcome the perceived inferiority of Blackness, and so African-descended individuals, no matter how Christian, were eternally consigned to second-class citizenship.

Our early ancestors' God-consciousness helped many of them discern the danger in these anti-Black sentiments; unfortunately, however, others fell victim to these ideologies/theologies and internalized anti-Blackness to their own physical and spiritual peril. Once independent Black churches and denominations began to arise, many of them retained anti-Black theological doctrines and tenets of slaveholders' churches. The effects of anti-Blackness and its resultant effect on theological tenets of visible sainthood, divine superiority, hereditary heathenism, and proslavery paternalism directly impacted worship practices and liturgical traditions of Black congregations. Some religious leaders of Black congregations superficially replicated acts and orders of worship from Eurocentric services with which they were familiar. Others fully adopted theological and doctrinal tenets of Calvinist (Puritan) and/or Anglican/Anglican-descended denominations and ordered worship services accordingly. The fallout of these decisions included losses and even negation of African heritage and Afrocentrism. Not only were performances of Africanisms/African retentions strongly discouraged or forbidden in many Black churches, African cosmological understandings of Creator, Spirit, and community were often abandoned in favor of Eurocentric ideologies, especially the adoption of much more individualistic, private, and economic understandings of Christianity. As we will see in the following chapter, Afrofuturism offers a much-needed counterpoint to these perspectives.

8

Worship and Music Through an Afrofuturist Lens

I am ready to consider a more expansive and cosmological liberation.
—Dr. Barbara Holmes[1]

WHAT CAN AFROFUTURISM OFFER the church, and particularly the Black church, to free our worship from the negative influences of death-dealing, anti-Black, and anti-liberationist ideologies? Afrofuturism directly addresses and counters narratives and ideologies that deny the worth of African and African-descended peoples and their viable and visible presence in the future. I contend that Afrofuturism's tools of imagination, inclusion, and improvisation can help us dismantle these ideologies (and the tangible ways they are built into our worship experiences), as well as help us construct healthier theological frameworks upon which life-giving worship can be based and experienced. Afrofuturism calls us to: 1) center African and African-descended cosmologies, theologies, and hermeneutics; 2) develop and implement liturgies that affirm and

---

1. Holmes, *Liberation and the Cosmos*, 258.

center Black peoples and our experiences; 3) employ elements of worship that affirm and center Black ancestral practices and characteristics; and 4) use imagination, improvisation, and adaptability to create new vistas for worship that employ and embrace mythmaking, conjure, and time-space exploration, and produce new metanarratives beyond race.

AFRICAN COSMOLOGY

Peter Paris asserts that "African societies on the continent have produced extremely complex cosmologies in their many and varied attempts to explain and relate the three realms of reality: spirit, history, and nature."[2] These cosmological worldviews served as broad and overarching concepts that infused and informed the daily lives of African communities. Religious and spiritual beliefs emanating from these worldviews found expression in both ritual worship and the mundane ordinariness of the workday.

African cosmological worldviews undergirded every aspect of the lives of her people and served as the foundation for the creation of Black worship in the New World. Scholars have noted several of these worldviews that many, if not most, African nations and peoples held in common. The first worldview is the belief in one supreme God, known across countries and cultures by many names, and who serves as "the High God" in a "monarchical polytheism"[3] with lesser deities. Mbiti writes, "God is outside and beyond His creation. On the other hand, He is personally involved in His creation, so that it is not outside of Him or His reach. God is thus simultaneously transcendent and immanent."[4] In some sense, the High God in many of these belief systems is not concerned or involved in the daily comings and goings of humanity, but delegates this work to lesser gods, each of whom has particular powers and abilities and is responsible for assisting humanity who request help

---

2. Paris, *Spirituality of African Peoples*, 34.
3. Wilmore, *Black Religion*, 20.
4. Mbiti, *African Religions and Philosophy*, 29.

in those areas. According to scholar Dwight Hopkins, other African religion practitioners do "believe in a God who cares" whom they refer to as "'the Compassionate One' or 'the God of pity' and who 'looks after the case of the poor man.'"[5] Hopkins continues, "God is a divinity of partiality to the victim; God sides with the political powerlessness of society's injured."[6] Beliefs in a God who possesses these attributes of compassion, caring, and concern for the poor would prove instrumental in the development of Black religion in the Americas.

A second worldview is communal solidarity in a system of relatedness known as kinship. The African concept of kinship does not extend merely horizontally to one's immediate family or close extended family, but also includes a vertical kinship with ancestors. Leonard Barrett notes, "The second major component of the African religious heritage in the New World is the belief that the ancestors have enormous influence over their descendants. This concept is universal among African peoples."[7] Though some have disparaged African veneration as "ancestor worship," Africans and people of African descent know that because ancestors are those who showed themselves during earthly existence to be helpful, they are still deserving of honor and respect. Moreover, Africans believe ancestors have a collective power that energizes the living and infuses daily life.

In addition to an esteem for ancestors, kinship includes interrelatedness with all creation. Costen asserts that "humanity is part of the created order, thus human beings are to exist in unity with one another and with all of creation. To be human means that one belongs to a family or community."[8] This worldview creates a theological construct that binds humanity together, out of which emerges a collective outlook for community—past, present, and future. There is a mutual interdependence that undergirds the entire structure upon which community is built. What happens to

5. Hopkins, *Shoes That Fit Our Feet*, 16–17.
6. Hopkins, *Shoes That Fit Our Feet*, 17.
7. Barrett, *Soul-Force*, 22.
8. Costen, *African American Christian Worship*, 9.

one happens to all; and what happens to all impacts the one. Decisions, therefore, are not just based on individual goals, desires, or happiness, but on what would benefit or harm the entire community. The principle of Ubuntu sums it up as: "I am because we are; and since we are, therefore, I am."[9]

Respect for nature as God's sacred creation is a third worldview that undergirds an African way of life. Mbiti notes that African peoples associate animals and plants with the concept of God, and often consider them sacred, eating some only after they are sacrificed in religious ceremonies.[10] Furthermore, the heavens carry God-meaning, along with weather phenomena such as rain, storms, and earthquakes. In other words, the entire universe exists in witness to God's power and beauty, through sign and symbol; therefore, humanity must respect nature as God's good gift and live holistically in harmony with it.[11] In conjunction with this regard and appreciation for nature is the need for humanity to internalize a relevant understanding of sacred cosmos. This concept involves several facets, including the African perspective that there is no separation between sacred and secular; all of life is sacred. Barrett states,

> The worldview of African peoples is best described as the vision of a cosmic harmony in which there exists a vital participation between animate (God, man) and inanimate things. That is to say, all Africans see a vital relationship of being between each individual and his descendants, his family, his brothers and sisters in the clan, his antecedents, and also his God—the ultimate source of being.[12]

A fourth African worldview that is both foundational and formational to Black worship is African wisdom—the creation and use of proverbs and folklore. As with the proverbs contained in the Hebrew Scriptures, African proverbs are not attributed to any

9. Mbiti, *African Religions and Philosophy*, 141.
10. Mbiti, *African Religions and Philosophy*, 50.
11. Karenga, "Black Religion," 273.
12. Barrett, *Soul-Force*, 17.

one source or elder; they exist as "the wisdom of the nation." They deal with various subjects, including humanity's relationship with God, one's moral behavior, and social virtues, and are used daily in a myriad of contexts. Folktales espouse the wisdom of elders, through narratives about God, lesser deities, the universe, humanity, animals, and the environment. These narratives contain and communicate a people's traditions, belief systems, and stories of origin regarding God and creation.

AFRICAN AND BLACK THEOLOGIES

How were these cosmologies, these primal worldviews, present in the theologies of Africans and their descendants during the antebellum period? For many scholars, the development of Black worship practices and the theologies that undergirded them is a syncretism of African beliefs and practices with European Christianity and folk religion that emerged out of the experience of enslavement.[13]

God

For peoples who were steeped in beliefs of God as the "High God," all-seeing, all-knowing, and all-powerful, an introduction to the Christian God as the "Most High" would have seemed an easy concept to grasp. What would have been more difficult to grasp was why the "High God" would have allowed them to arrive at such a horrific place and under such brutal oppression as enslavement. What also would have been illogical and inconsistent was how the Christian God was presented by their white captors as one who justified their bondage and maltreatment. Hopkins notes that "despite the apparent immortality of the slave system, black chattel persisted in a faith in the God of freedom . . . and simply refused

---

13. See Raboteau, *Slave Religion*; Herskovitz, *Myth of the Negro Past*; and Frazier, *Negro Church*.

to accept white theology."[14] The African/African American theological construct of God from the perspective of enslaved persons was an image of one who, despite their circumstances, was still their protector, defender, judge, and potential liberator. Though the "High God" might still have been considered transcendent and "far off," in their daily struggles for humanity, God was immanent and "nearby." For enslaved Africans and their descendants, God was intimately concerned with and a major participant in their quest for justice and liberation.

Jesus

How would *AfricansinAmerica* have perceived the notion of Jesus Christ, as Son of God? Raboteau asserts that, because of their understanding of lesser gods or divinities who worked as intermediaries for the "High God," enslaved Africans would have readily accepted Jesus as God's divine representative.[15] Furthermore, stories of Jesus as suffering servant and sacrificial lamb would have resonated deeply with those who daily bore the brunt of physical torture and suffering. Just as significant is the enslaved African's understanding of Jesus as the Resurrected One, victorious, not just over certain individuals who betrayed and killed him, but over systems of oppression that betrayed and killed him. The theological assertion that Jesus wouldn't "die no mo" assured the enslaved community that evil kingdoms, indeed the kingdom of Satan—as represented by white slaveholders—had been defeated by Jesus's death and resurrection.

Holy Spirit

Though enslaved persons, particularly those who were African-born and first-generation Americans, might not have understood Trinitarian concepts of God nor believed that only three

---

14. Hopkins, *Shoes That Fit Our Feet*, 23.
15. Raboteau, *Slave Religion*, 127.

gods—Father, Son, and Holy Spirit—were sufficient to carry out the Creator's plans, they would have understood the character and nature of the Holy Spirit. For the enslaved, the slaveholders' system of conversion rang hollow and led to the development of what they believed was a more authentic catechesis known as "getting religion" or the "seekin" journey or experience. According to George Cummings, "Some slaves had visions, others shouted and walked, and still others bore witness to the creative power of the Spirit. The Spirit possessed the physical being of the slaves, and consequently they shouted; spoke of great visions of God, heaven, or freedom; and engaged in physical activity that manifested the Spirit's presence."[16] Africans and their descendants familiar with spirit possession in the African sense would have perceived these experiences as authentic and normative for a worship participant. The work of the Spirit in Black antebellum worship was to intensify and enhance the worship and the more-hoped-for conversion experiences of the enslaved, as well as provide a liberative sense of joy, amid unbearable sorrow. Though definitely not identical to the African understanding of spirit possession, the indwelling of the Spirit in Black antebellum worship was just as efficacious and transformative for the participant and would find its way into all liturgical practices of the *invisible institution*, and beyond.

CENTERING WOMANIST ETHICS AND HERMENEUTICS

Katie Geneva Cannon, mother of womanist ethics, laid the groundwork for constructing alternative sites of ethical and theological authority that inform a more liberative liturgical and theological paradigm. Her areas of focus assist us in seeing the ways worship has been beset by androcentric, patriarchal, and ableist patterns and give us a framework within which to question, evaluate, reform, and replace those patterns that are death dealing and antithetical to the goal of a "holistic justice agenda in private and

---

16. Cummings, "Slave Narratives," 34.

public spheres."[17] Womanist ethicist Stacey Floyd-Thomas describes how the concept of womanism emerged:

> By various levels of inspiration, Black women could bear witness to the truth of their surroundings and situations. With changed names and changed minds, these Black women took hold of an emerging consciousness that not only provided a new outlook on life but also ushered forth a new epistemology. An epistemology, or way of knowing, that took the experience of Black women as normative.[18]

Womanist God-talk examines and critiques our theological and religious doctrines and beliefs, using its four tenets to construct alternate theologies that employ liberative womanist ethics. Womanist biblical hermeneutics requires, among other tasks, reclaiming neglected histories and stories of black peoples within divergent biblical traditions and analyzing and documenting the effects of biblical interpretation on African and African diasporic peoples.[19] Womanist scholar Delores Williams offers an *identification-ascertainment* hermeneutic model which involves three modes of inquiry: subjective, communal, and objective.[20] These modes involve analyses of self- and communal identification with biblical texts and socio-political-cultural affiliations held because of said identifications. It also observes who has and has not been identified in the biblical text and how that impacts individuals and communities.

Womanist ethics and hermeneutics seek to center and affirm Black women's histories and experiences and how these impact biblical exegesis, theological assertions, and beliefs, and how what is preached and taught to Black peoples about the Bible and religious experience influences and impacts them, positively or negatively. Hermeneutics of suspicion and an ethic and hermeneutic of incarnation help mitigate the denial of personhood that victimizes Black

---

17. Allen, *Womanist Theology of Worship*, 313.
18. Floyd-Thomas, "Writing for Our Lives," 3.
19. Martin, "Womanist Biblical Interpretation."
20. Williams, *Sisters in the Wilderness*, 149.

peoples in religious experiences while affirming their presence and personhood in texts, as well as in contemporary worship spaces.

LITURGIES

Employing these various ethics and hermeneutics of liberation, suspicion, and incarnation in liturgical theology, the studying, writing, and doing of it, has the potential to produce richer, more meaningful, holistic, and transformative worship experiences for all attendees. Exploring, analyzing, and critiquing liturgical elements through these lenses serve to assist the worshiper, worship leader, and worship planner in four distinct ways. First, engaging in this work makes those who are worshiping and planning worship reflect and ask questions about how and why the service is ordered in a particular manner, questions that might not have arisen in previous instances. Second, it creates opportunities for extensive dialogue between clergy and laity. As these ethics and hermeneutics are applied to liturgical elements, there is the potential for fruitful, albeit uncomfortable, conversations, theological discussions, exegetical questions, and opportunities for participants to engage in worship planning as a way of employing new understandings in worship, as a result. Third, it potentially inspires further study and research. Introducing new concepts in an inclusive, nonthreatening communal forum often stimulates the desire to know more about a given topic. Last, engaging in dialogue strengthens communal fellowship and congregational engagement. Hearing different perspectives and personal narratives, sharing stories of life-changing events, and confessing one's struggles to understand particular concepts and beliefs, again, in nonthreatening spaces, with the common goal of producing life-giving, life-affirming liturgies that *every body* can proclaim without marginalization transform a church into the body of Christ.

Afrofuturist liturgies that emerge from the work of intentional and communal engagement with liberation and womanist theologies, ethics, and hermeneutics have the potential to dismantle death-dealing religious ideologies that pervade many current worship spaces and do harm to a multitude of communities. The use of ancestral, liberative theologies and spirituality, removal/revision of exclusive and anti-Black language, and the affirmation and invitation of full embodiment of all persons requires a great deal of effort by a committed group of people willing to wrestle with church tradition, embedded theologies, and preconceived notions and biases around what constitutes orthodoxy (right belief) and orthopraxy (right practice). There *will* be pushback, but if faith communities envision their futures as healthy, holistic, and thriving spaces where transformation into God's beloved community is the goal, it is necessary work.

THE AFROFUTURIST NATURE OF ANCESTRAL MUSIC LINEAGES

How can Afrofuturism help us discover, uncover, and recover the meaning and significance of our ancestral music lineages? Afrofuturism calls us to recover, uncover, and discover the ancestral roots of our worship that affirmed, supported, and utilized the spiritual technologies of imagination, adaptability, and improvisation to propel us forward into our collective futures. It can help us transform our churches and the communities we serve into the beloved community Jesus continually preached and taught about and into which he calls us daily.

SPIRITUAL TECHNOLOGY

What is spiritual technology? How does something come to be considered a spiritual technology? To help us understand this concept, we turn first to Michaela Leslie-Rule, Ron Ragin, and T. Carlis Roberts, three scholar/artist practitioners who head up the Spiritual Technologies Project (STP), which uses research, performance, and workshops to study, create, and disseminate practices which have the potential to transform communities. STP offers this definition of spiritual technologies:

> In contrast to mechanical or digital devices, spiritual technologies are repeated cultural practices meant to alter the mind, body, or spirit of an individual or community. They are developed and cultivated for the explicit purpose of connecting people with each other and with their environment. In the process, all is transformed, linked, and expanded.[21]

According to the editor of ReligionLink, "In scholarly circles, 'spiritual technology' is used to refer to any practice believed to enhance a person's religious practices or identification."[22] Practices including water immersions, meditation in specialized locations, and prayer recitations to aid those seeking a deeper connection with the Divine to attain desired states of consciousness or wisdom. These practices are not new; indeed, for millennia, individuals and communities have used developments in media, travel, and information technology to broaden and expand their religious and faith horizons.

How does African/Black ancestral music function as spiritual technology? Using the definitions given, ancestral music is a form of spiritual technology because: 1) it enhances a person's or, in this case, a people's religious devotion and identification; 2) the singing and playing of ancestral music are repeated cultural practices meant to alter the mind, body, or spirit of an individual or community; 3) it was developed and cultivated for the explicit purposes of connecting people with each other and with their environment. Further, the music of our ancestors was created through and, in its performance inspires, imagination, adaptability, and improvisation, which are hallmarks of spiritual technologies.

We will explore how each of these ancestral genres historically and contemporarily functions and has the potential to future the Black church through the lenses of the four common themes of Black worship: survival, resistance, deliverance and liberation, and affirmation and joy.

---

21. Spiritual Technologies Project, "About," para. 2.
22. Editor, "Spiritual Technologies," para. 6.

SPIRITUALS

The creation of spirituals arose initially out of an immediate response to the brutal, horrific circumstances of enslavement. Often, the only way enslaved persons had to cope with these conditions was to cry out, either in solitude or communally in the br(hush) arbor. Making music out of one's sorrow, anguish, or despair was a technique of survival, first, because it reminded our ancestors that they were still alive, still human, amid inhumane treatment. Lifting voices meant that the music had not been beaten out of them, that enough life remained to raise a song, however solemn. Within the lyrics and music of spirituals was the spiritual technology to alter one's mental, emotional, and even physical state of being while being strengthened to endure another day until freedom came.

Spirituals also were tools of resistance against the injustice of enslavement. As their lyrics spoke the Divine's name, the singing conjured up the Spirit of God, empowering and strengthening them to live, despite the oppressor's determination to kill them. Calling persons to worship, alerting people of possible opportunities to escape, singing about one's oppressors in code—all of these were strategies of resistance, ways to fight back communally, to take agency even when there appeared to be none available to them.

How, then, can spirituals as a spiritual technology future the church? They provide the same tools of survival and resistance now that they did then. Though we are hundreds of years removed from chattel slavery, Black peoples across the globe, and particularly in America, still suffer from the terrors and injustice of white supremacy. We still live with the historical effects of enslavement, including societal marginalization and the racist backlash that raises its head whenever Black peoples are determined to thrive. While these songs may be ancestral, the lyrics and music still conjure up the Spirit of God in God's people, and empower us to fight on, individually and communally, against terror, brutality, and the ever-present notions that Black people are inhuman, or, at best, subhuman.

Many will counter that we are no longer enslaved, that we have the power to do whatever is in our best interests, that singing spirituals is best left to Black History programs once a year. But I contend that, while we may not be physically enslaved, we still suffer from the legacies of enslavement and are facing a future where many are working diligently to undo all the gains that Black peoples have made. Indeed, in America, Black people have never known a time when we have not been endangered by racist ideologues determined to turn back the clock and return us to a time of enslavement. Spirituals, as an Afrofuturist spiritual technology, counter death-dealing narratives with lyrics that affirm Black humanity, spirituality, and sacrality, and provide avenues for continued lyrical and musical imagination and improvisation that help us envision ourselves beyond current realities.

According to Afrofuturist scholar Ytasha Womack, "Afrofuturism's central symbol is a 'looking back to go forward' . . . best exemplified by the *sankofa* image, signifying a way to the future by remembering the past." Womack asserts that, for the Afrofuturist, "futures and histories are constantly informing one another."[23] Spirituals embody the *Sankofan* concept of looking back to go forward, providing a direct link musically, liturgically, emotionally, and psychologically to Mother Africa. As we have stated, African cosmologies, theologies, musics, and liturgies provided our ancestors and continue to provide us with liberative, imaginative, and spiritual power to strengthen and move ourselves and communities forward, despite circumstances to the contrary.

HYMNOLOGY

Lined/Metered Hymns

Other than spirituals, there is no congregational music that connects African and North American descendants of Africa more than lined hymns. While the lyrics of lined hymns most often arose from the pens of English clerics, the melodies and harmonies are purely African. Built on a foundation of pentatonic and other African modal scales, the use of flatted sixth and seventh notes, the

---

23. Womack, "I Came to Africa," 50.

prevalence of intervals built on fourths and fifths, and wavering between major and minor harmonies are all indicative of African vocal sound. Further, the performance of lined hymns bespeaks an African spirituality through call-and-response, improvisation, and congregational connection. There is no such thing as a soloist in a lined hymn; there is a leader who calls out the line, either spoken or sung, however, the person is not viewed singularly, but as part of the collective voice of the congregation.

The congregational nature of lined hymns is at the heart of this genre as a spiritual technology. To sing a lined hymn collectively is to experience simultaneously a transformation of the communal mind, soul, and spirit. As the song tempo accelerates, one can feel a shifting in the voices, surging forward, adding harmonies over and above the melody, mirroring the spiritual escalation taking place within the hearts and minds of the group. The experience recalls ancestral encounters in the praise house, where enslaved Africans lifted their voices as one without shame or hesitation, calling up/conjuring the Spirit to come and dwell among them. As the deacons prayed following the singing, the congregation would continue to hum and moan the hymn, singing/calling out, "Lord, have mercy" and "I done died one time, I ain't gon' die no more," referencing the liberation received with a new life in Christ, while also alluding to their belief they would be free one day in the present realm.

The choice of lyrics for lined hymns also references African cosmologies. Enslaved Africans and their descendants would not have chosen every hymn heard in the slaveholders' churches, but would select those that affirmed African cosmological understandings of God and of themselves. Popular hymn texts included "I Love the Lord, He Heard My Cry," "Father, I Stretch My Hands to Thee," "A Charge to Keep I Have," and "Guide Me, O Thou Great Jehovah." Each of these speaks to a theological understanding of a personal God who met the needs of those who sought God, and to whom they could call on in times of trial, distress, and doubt. They would also improvise their own lyrics that spoke to their specific spiritual location, such as "Before this time another year / I may be dead and gone / I'll let you know before I go / what will become of me" and "I know I am a child of God / although I move so slow / I'll wait until the Spirit comes / and move at God's command." The extemporaneity of these lyrics exemplifies the use of spiritual technologies in worship, acknowledging common humanity, mortality, and exhibiting trust in God's timing amid the immediacy of need.

Traditional Hymns

While traditional hymnody typically follows musical patterns of Western choral literature, it still serves lyrically as a spiritual guide for the Black church. The primary gift of hymnody is theological instruction and nurture. There are few, if any, other places where people gather as a collective regularly to sing what they believe. Hymns teach theology communally, as we sing from a canon of songs compiled by those entrusted with a congregation's theological understanding. Additionally, singing hymns provides historic ties with those who have gone before us, ancestors who affirmed within faith communities the same beliefs we now affirm with the same hymns. Afrofuturism helps us look back as we look forward, singing the hymns of our progenitors, while adapting lyrics to include inclusive, affirming language, and penning new hymns that reflect cultural sensibilities and theological viewpoints of a twenty-first-century postmodern society.

The Black church has a canon of hymnody that extends beyond denominational boundaries. Most historically Black denominations have their own hymnals, but within most of these, one will find many hymns held in common with one another. As the genre of hymnody developed, there were hymns that Black congregations gravitated toward for several reasons. First, as mentioned previously, the lyrics reflected African cosmologies about the nearness of God and God's intimate care of those in need. Second, these hymns contain easily sung melodies and harmonies that have become well loved by Black congregations. Third, these hymns can be rhythmically adapted to new tempi, allowing churches to modernize them with rhythm instruments and body percussion.

It is also important to mention here that the Black church's modern canon of hymnody includes songs that were not originally penned as hymns. Many gospel songs have been canonized as hymns because of their enduring and widely held popularity. While these songs were not written expressly for use by congregations, they are so well known that those compiling hymnals have begun including them so that congregations can have access to the written compositions and sing them accurately. Some of these include James Cleveland's "Peace, Be Still," Richard Smallwood's "Total Praise," Esther Watanabe's "I Will Bless Thee, O Lord," and Winston Rodney's "Praise Him," popularized by the New Jersey Mass Choir. Again, this is Afrofuturist in concept because these songs, which were composed using the rudiments of African/Black music theory, are now being sung by the descendants of those who created these musical patterns, and being used to propel the church forward spiritually.

Gospels

Like spirituals and lined hymns, the origin of gospel music was a spiritual technology within itself. As mentioned in the chapter on gospel music, this genre grew out of the need to express one's personal feelings about faith, trials, and the presence of God through the vicissitudes of life. Gospel music gave singers the ability to alter their mental, emotional, and spiritual states within the context of worship experiences. They did not have to hide or find alternate places of worship, but could openly groan, cry, weep, wail, and shout as they were singing in worship, and experience collectively an ecstatic spiritual outpouring vocally and instrumentally. Gospel music was and is Afrofuturist because it developed out of a need to be authentically Black in a time and in spaces where Blackness was not often welcomed, even by other Black worshipers. The rapid rise of independent and storefront churches in urban centers reflected the determination of Black worshipers, particularly in northern states, to create liberative spaces where they could worship as charismatically as they desired.

Worship and Music Through an Afrofuturist Lens

The use of electronic instruments, including Hammond B3 organs (originally designed for rhythm and blues bands), drum kits, and brass and wind instruments previously reserved for secular groups, further identifies gospel music as Afrofuturist. Though the line between sacred and secular was historically faint in African-descended worship spaces, in many denominational churches the line had been made more visible after the turn of the twentieth century. But in churches where gospel music was foundational to and in worship, the instrumentality often kept the lines quite blurred. It rarely mattered, though, because the lyrics were undoubtedly Christian, and those who were singing were clear to whom and about whom they were singing.

Musically, gospel music is Afrofuturist because it thrives on improvisation and extemporaneity. One need only listen to or watch a choir in action as the band begins its lively intro. Hands clap, bodies rock, and singers call out in joy as they prepare to sing the opening line. As the choir sings, they follow the choir director, who determines the order of the song, deciding at a moment's notice whether to return to the beginning or continue to the refrain. Once the choir reaches the vamp, various singers may take turns in a call-and-response style, the band may improvise new chordal and harmonic structures and rhythm patterns. There may be technological experimentation in the form of click tracks, instrumental sounds, video, or stage lighting designs, all under the supervision of the director and with the understanding that whatever is happening must serve the music and the music must minister to the people.

What is also decidedly Afrofuturist about gospel music is that each song, in some sense, is both a personal and a collective testimony of faith. A prevalent theme in the genre is looking back at what God has done as an indicator of God's faithfulness and ability to do for the believer again. Lyrics often recount biblical narratives, particularly about the life of Jesus, and testify to how the Divine continues to show up in the lives of believers, which offers an assurance that God is and will continue to be with them and sustain them. Other songs contain lyrics that speak directly to the immediacy of the singer's or group's need or offer of praise. Even in these songs, there prevails the sense that God cares for and keeps God's children. These statements of assurance are Afrofuturist in the sense that the singer or group affirms their individual and the group's collective future, both here and in the life to come.

NEW VISTAS

Afrofuturism calls, moves, and propels its proponents to create, through the tools and spiritual technologies of imagination, improvisation, and adaptability. Envisioning Black people, the Black church, Black theologies, and Black worship in and into the future requires looking beyond the present toward possibilities and even previously considered impossibilities. It also requires the dismantling of hegemonic and racist structures that preclude Black peoples from utilizing ancestral languages, religious practices, modes of communication and thought, and other technologies that contain powers to heal, repair, restore, and renew practitioners. As a pastor in a Black mainline denomination, I know how uncomfortable many people become when talking about ancestral traditions, but it is because we have been taught for centuries that anything from Africa, particularly of a religious nature, is demonic. Our ancestors were stripped of and denied the right to employ, recover, or research any element of their African heritage, whether it was language, music, instruments, religious beliefs and practices, medicinal knowledge, artifacts, signs, symbols, or identities. Any attempt to remember or re-member one's Africanness was swiftly and severely punished. Those who had been shamans, medicine people, or spiritualists were killed or seriously debilitated on African and American coasts or isolated from others.

Once Africans and their descendants began to be catechized into Christianity, anything of African origin or derivation was castigated as evil or demonic. Eurocentric/Anglo theologies, built on white supremacist, anti-Black foundations developed from early patristic writings, reports of explorers, pseudoscientific assertions, and notions of colonial superiority had a most deleterious effect on enslaved Africans and their descendants. To be African was to be considered nonhuman, or at best, subhuman, unworthy of salvation, and destined for hell. African rites and rituals, observed by explorers and captors, were deemed the work of savages, beasts, cannibals, and were considered devil worship. Theories regarding African racial inferiority, including Zurara's "beast theory," Jean Bodin's "heat theory," Montesquieu's "climate theory," and George Best's "curse theory," among others, fed and underscored anti-Black sentiments, theologies, societal codes, and laws that contributed to the marginalization and oppression of *AfricansinAmerica*.

These theories and subsequent theologies and perceptions still exist, negatively impacting twenty-first-century Africans and African-descended peoples around the world. And because of these histories and pervasive legacies, Black Christians are often fearful of and hesitant to acknowledge Africanisms, African retentions, and African ancestral religious practices that were and, to some extents, still are present in worship in many Black congregations. I've experienced Black people questioning and/or disparaging the pouring of libation, use of African names for God, calling the names of ancestors, use of the word "Ase,"[24] African drumming and dancing, and other elements that reflect African worship traditions. When asked why they are so hesitant to participate or why they do not approve of these elements, responses vary from being fearful that certain African elements mirror the practice of witchcraft or open up portals to demonic spirits, the elements being used are not compatible with Christian teaching, being afraid of divine punishment and/or going to hell for heresy or heterodoxy, and/or ignorance about particular traditions and their meanings. However, when asked to provide proof of the presence of witchcraft or demonic spirits, or to provide scriptural references that evince incompatibility with Christian teaching, I've not known a single instance where individuals were able to substantiate their

24. "Ase/Ashe" is a Yoruba word that means "It is so" or "So be it." It is often thought to be an African parallel to the English word, "Amen." However, "Ase/Ashe" has a deeper meaning in that the person who says it is also affirming that they commit their spiritual and physical energy to helping make whatever is being spoken about a reality.

claims. Then, often the refrain I hear is, "I don't want to take any chances with my salvation." Afrofuturism, however, invites us to recapture an ancestral vision of communal salvation.

One of the negative legacies of Eurocentric theologies, particularly as practiced in North America, is the individualistic, pietistic view of salvation. Evangelicalism, as it arose during the Great Awakenings of the seventeenth through the nineteenth centuries, proffered the theological idea of a personal relationship with Jesus that saved one's soul and ensured one's entrance into heaven in the afterlife. Further, this model underscored the separation of sacred and secular, the dichotomy between the evil flesh and the divine spirit. Unfortunately, Africans and their descendants gravitated toward this model of salvation to the detriment of their own communities. Spirituality took a back seat to religiosity; communing with the Divine fell out of favor while the public performance of personal holiness and orthodoxy took center stage. Many Black worshiping communities have not recovered from this paradigm, which has resulted in unhealthy, inauthentic worship experiences based on false dichotomies and death-dealing doctrinal trauma. Afrofuturism offers us new ways to recover authentic and communal ancestral spirituality, through the spiritual practices and technologies of mythmaking, Conjure, and time exploration.

Mythmaking

> [Myths are] the best way—sometimes the only way—of conveying truths that would otherwise remain inexpressible. We have come from God and inevitably the myths woven by us, though they contain error, reflect a splintered fragment of the true light, the eternal truth that is with God.[25]

These words, attributed to J. R. R. Tolkien, author of *The Lord of the Rings* trilogy and other fantasy novels, speak to the power of mythmaking. Here, Tolkien makes the claim that myths have a

---

25. Magis Center, "Purpose of a Myth," para. 6.

deeper meaning than the stories or narratives they weave; they provide the mythmaker and listener/reader an entryway into eternal realms, a view of the transcendent that the natural world cannot contain and often hinders us from seeing. Another quote, from a course offered in the University of Virginia College of Arts and Sciences, helps us understand why mythmaking is so important:

> Myths and stories have the power to shape our sense of ourselves, our world, and the meaning of life; we tell, retell, and reshape them in order to discover who we are, explore the choices we face, and imagine how we should live.[26]

In chapter 3, we examined how spirituals operated as folklore, providing coping strategies and serving as theological and ethical affirmations of faith for *AfricansinAmerica*. But, for this discussion, I would like especially to revisit Dr. Cannon's assertion that spirituals were "the indispensable device that slaves . . . used to transmit a worldview fundamentally different from and opposed to that of slaveholders."[27] The language in that statement paints a different picture about the origin and use of spirituals than as a coping mechanism. Here, Dr. Cannon refers to them as being able to transmit a fundamentally different worldview—that is an Afrofuturist spiritual technology that has transformative power for the contemporary Black church. The stories we tell, through the interpretation and hermeneutical exposition of biblical texts, the retelling of ancestral memories, songs we sing, prayers we pray, and the testimonies we give, all contain the ability to help us create and re-create our worlds into what we want them to be. Whether we believe the Bible to be the inerrant word of God, recollections of actual events, metanarratives of a particular people in particular places, allegories, myths, or fables, the ways we interpret texts and interweave them with the sacred texts which are our actual lives build worlds in which we live either free or bound.

---

26. Halvorson-Taylor, "Mythmaking."
27. Cannon, *Katie's Canon*, 35.

What narratives are we telling, remembering, and re-membering? Are they stories that honor sacred memory and help define and determine communal destinies? Do the narratives we believe define us as a people and/or faith community lift us up and help us to see ourselves in futures that are bright and hope filled? Or are they filled with despair or resignation to a joyless future where others are still in charge of our existence? Are our narratives replete with angry rhetoric about oppression and injustice, lacking any luminous vision or prescient inspiration to counter the negative impacts and fatigue of having to do constant battle? I am not suggesting that we create a false narrative that glosses over reality, but that we engage ancestral spiritual technologies that are already present within us and our communities to co-construct with the Divine the future that we desire. Part of that construction is envisioning ourselves there—to *be* it you first have to *see* it. The choices are ours to make with the stories we tell, and we can make liberative exegetical and hermeneutic choices or remain bound by theologies and doctrines that continue to kill us and our communities.

What new worldviews are we transmitting with our worship? Are they inclusive of all creation and especially of all peoples, regardless of identity? Are our worship spaces safe for all stories? Do they honor all mythmaking or just that of accepted members of the community? Are we willing to engage in new mythmaking that invites imagination to posit new theories and outcomes of ancient stories, or will we remain afraid and allow our fears to limit what we deem as possible? Does our music employ *Sankofan* methods, bringing our past into view while propelling us forward with lyrics, melodies, harmonies, and rhythms that bespeak spiritual awareness, creativity, and ingenuity to co-create with the Divine?

Conjure

I hesitated to include Conjure in this book, not because I don't believe it is a spiritual practice or technology, but because I know that the word itself is loaded with multiple meanings, many of which are viewed negatively by Christian believers. However, I

Worship and Music Through an Afrofuturist Lens

believe a conversation, albeit limited, about the history and practices of Conjure by our ancestors is necessary if we want to avail ourselves of Afrofuturist spiritual technologies that can free and future Black people.

It has been well established that Africans who arrived on North American shores brought their religious memories, including worshiping traditions, rites, and rituals. As previously mentioned, some might have already been introduced to Coptic or Ethiopian Orthodox Christianity. The indigenous religions and practices they brought with them remained in their consciousness, even amid systematic attempts by slaveholders to strip enslaved Africans of their beliefs. African cosmological and theological worldviews were not dichotomized into sacred and secular; rather, they reflected an understanding of the world that was holistic and acknowledged the sacredness of all creation. Though Western conceptualizations of African religious practices compartmentalized them as either religion, magic, or witchcraft, the lines cannot be so easily demarcated, particularly since African indigenous religions held that all of life was governed by a spiritual reality. Comprehension and internalization of the sacred cosmos are what give meaning and purpose to life, and one must perceive oneself as part of the divine creation that exists in the natural world and evinces itself through cosmic rhythm. As scholar John Mbiti asserts, "African peoples are aware of mystical power in the universe. This power is ultimately from God, but in practice it is inherent in, or comes from or through physical objects and spiritual beings."[28]

What is Conjure and what were some of its purposes among enslaved Africans and their descendants? Yvonne Chireau defines Conjure as a "tradition in which spiritual power is invoked for various purposes, such as healing, protection, and self-defense."[29] While those who practiced Conjure did so for various reasons, most often it was in response to those in the community who came seeking assistance with personal matters. In their practices of Conjure, spiritualists provided reassurance, comfort, clarity, and

28. Mbiti, *African Religions and Philosophy*, 197.
29. Chireau, *Black Magic*, 12.

avenues through which persons could achieve mental, emotional, physical, and spiritual strength, healing, and restoration. However, one of the most important uses of Conjure during the antebellum period (and why I believe an understanding of Conjure is essential for the future of *AfricansinAmerica*) was as a deterrent to slaveholders who often used violent means to enact their will upon enslaved Africans. Many historians note the perceived efficacy of conjurers to stabilize, subdue, and even overpower (at least temporarily) slaveholders who sought to physically harm or otherwise oppress enslaved individuals. Dozens, if not hundreds, of recollections exist that recount how the practice of Conjure was employed to empower slave revolts, provide protection from whippings and floggings, or prevent persons from being sold away.[30]

What is important as well to note is that while Conjure and Christianity might have seemed or been reported to be antithetical to one another, the distinctions were not always perfectly clear. We must remember that enslaved Africans were not catechized into American Christianity in any systematic way, especially in the southern colonies, until the late seventeenth and early eighteenth centuries. Before this, enslaved Africans practiced whatever religious beliefs they could remember individually or within the confines of the *invisible institution*. Once allowed into the slaveholders' churches or allowed a preacher in an accepted gathering of enslaved persons, *AfricansinAmerica* did not completely relinquish their African gods or religious practices. Rather, they developed a syncretized Afro-Baptist sacred cosmos, an Africanized Christianity which incorporated aspects of their African heritage and belief systems with and into this new religion.[31] According to Chireau and others, religious leaders in enslaved communities often included both Christian ministers and Conjurers, who were sometimes the same people.[32] Some had been designated from birth as "special," or "sighted"; others claimed to be called to the

---

30. See Rucker, "Conjure"; Blassingame, *Slave Community*; and W. Brown, "Narrative."

31. Sobel, *Trabelin' On*, 80.

32. Chireau, *Black Magic*, 14.

office of spiritualist or conjurer. Some navigated the boundaries of Christianity and Conjure by asserting they practiced Conjure only to heal people, not for any negative or evil purpose. Others directly professed Christianity and saw no conflict between their Christian beliefs and practices and Conjure. As Donald Waters succinctly states, "Black Americans were able to move between Conjure and Christianity because both were perceived as viable systems for accessing the supernatural world, and each met needs that the other did not."[33]

What I contend is most helpful about Conjure to the contemporary Black church is its roots in resistance and its ability to empower Black peoples in concrete, life-giving ways. Enslaved Africans and their descendants who often felt they had no recourse or ability to fight the daily injustices they endured were transformed by the spiritual power which came forth in the practice and experience of conjuration. The Spirit, which was "worked up" by those who believed in the Spirit's power, indwelt those present and transformed them into spiritually powerful conduits, ready to do the difficult and necessary work of liberation for themselves and their communities. And before we contest these practices because they are "demonic," let us examine our own worship practices.

Do we not also "work up" the Spirit in our worship services through congregational, choral, and instrumental music, prayer, and praise? I have heard the praying of prayers that became revelatory prophetic utterances under the unction of the Holy Spirit. I have witnessed numerous worship services where the worship leader or preacher stated that "we need music to 'shift' the atmosphere" and "I need the choir to get us ready to hear a message from on high." I have experienced the resultant charismatic outpouring of the Spirit that evinced itself among those gathered through glossolalia and holy dancing. Are these not the result of "working up" or "conjuring up" the Spirit? I dare say these are similar, if not identical, to the experiences our ancestors witnessed. The major difference is that today's contemporary charismatic service rarely results in politically motivated uprisings to

---

33. Waters, *Strange Ways*, 43.

secure liberation. Perhaps that is because we have lost the ancestral connection to Conjure in favor of a safe, individual, temporary visitation of the Spirit that makes us feel good while leaving us basically unchanged. Many churches hold "deliverance" services, but who is getting delivered and from what? What communities are experiencing deliverance from poverty, lack of educational access, unemployment and underemployment, redlining and other unfair housing practices, voter suppression, and mass incarceration because of these services? We need to recover the ancestral, life-giving spiritual technology of Conjure.

Time-Space Exploration

In the church, we refer to two understandings of time, *chronos* and *kairos*. *Chronos* time is the linear progression of measured time that occurs sequentially and can be quantified, such as time on a clock or a calendar. *Kairos* time is defined as "a time when conditions are right for the accomplishment of a crucial action; the opportune and decisive moment."[34] In *kairos*, God breaks into human history through people and events that change the world, e.g., the birth and resurrection of Jesus, the raising of Lazarus, and the birth of the church at Pentecost. *Kairos* time is not linear or temporal, but eschatological and eternal.

Afrofuturism proposes a different understanding of time than both *chronos* and *kairos* and reflects an Africanist view of time, keeping in the consciousness past, present, and future dimensions. In Afrofuturist thinking, time is cyclical and recursive, not linear. As Jayna Brown writes in *Black Utopias*, "We do not experience existence as a succession of static states, in linear progression. Instead, conscious experience of time is a constant swirl, with no linear coordinates, no beginning, middle, or end."[35] Time in the consciousness of Africans and their descendants is never limited to the here and now; it always sees and considers what has gone

---

34. *Merriam Webster Online*, s.v. "kairos," https://www.merriam-webster.com/dictionary/kairos.

35 J. Brown, *Black Utopias*, 171.

before and how what has happened might affect or impact what is to come. Life for most Black peoples is almost always viewed through the prism of past events, used as a lens or filter through which to understand and navigate what is occurring in the present. Where African-descended peoples have often struggled is how to envision a gradual and significantly sustained future.

Black peoples in the diaspora inherited this conceptual framework of time, including the struggle to see ourselves in an extended future. Our ancestors who were brought to these shores could not fathom that their lives would become daily tests for survival, so it was even more difficult to consider what the future (beyond an eschatological vision of freedom) might look like. Life was to be lived in the immediate moment, as that was all they had; tomorrow could bring separation or death. Many did not even dare to hope for freedom, choosing instead to embrace whatever peace they could eke out from their current situations.

This African concept of time was reflected in the music our ancestors produced—spirituals, blues, lined hymns, chants, and hymn choruses were typically created in the immediacy of performance improvisation, individually and communally. The lyrics evinced the cyclical nature of life, from birth to death, and how it was an ever-revolving circle of interwoven and interrelated events. Further, the eschatological vision of liberation ran through many of the songs, especially those with religious themes, which helped subvert the linear understanding of time foisted on them by the system of enslavement. This subversive understanding of time undergirded worship in the *invisible institution*, praise/pray's houses, and independent churches not bound by time or respectability constraints. Ancestral music infused Black worship in these contexts, permeating their atmospheres with sounds of spiritual, physical, mental, emotional, and *time* freedom.

An Afrofuturist hermeneutic of time both informs and benefits from ancestral music. Contemporary faith communities can employ ancestral music in efforts to subvert the capitalist, consumer-driven society we live in that pushes us to fill every moment with productivity, lest we be perceived as lazy, unenterprising, and ultimately, unworthy of being able to control our own lives. When attempts are made to assimilate into the dominant culture by diminishing or eliminating ancestral music and worship traditions, African-descended faith communities often lose the authenticity that makes worship meaningful and transformative. Ancestral music reminds us that "working up" the Spirit and creating an atmosphere in worship where the Holy Spirit descends and indwells the people takes time, not just *chronos* time, but more significantly, *kairos* and Afrofuturist time.

What we can see from our exploration of Afrofuturism as it relates to worship and each of these ancestral genres is a clear connection with our African past and a look into our *Afrofuture*. Afrofuturism calls for the Black church to remember and recover the best of its African and African American history, cosmology, and theology, rediscover the richness and spiritual depth of our sacred music, and combine these elements to create Afrofuturist worship encounters with the one who was, who is, and who will be. In this, Black/African peoples can be assured that we who were, *are*, and will also continue to be.

Epilogue

I want to be ready
I want to be ready
I want to be ready
to walk in Jerusalem just like John.

—Traditional Spiritual

At the 2024 commencement exercises of Clark Atlanta University (CAU!), the speaker, Dr. Daniel P. Black, CAU faculty member and nationally recognized and awarded author, began his address with the refrain, "Here they come, y'all, here they come!" He continued,

> The dream of the slave, the hope of the angels, the promise of the ancestors, the answers to grandmama's prayers, the guarantee of granddaddy's work; here they come, y'all, here they come! . . . See, some of y'all sitting here, people doubted you, but here you are anyway . . . you got discouraged, you almost dropped out, you got frustrated, you almost let it go . . . you told God, "I can't do this no more." . . . Anywhere you go, where the Holy Ghost resides, there will be magic, there will be promise, there will be possibilities.[1]

1. Black, "Commencement Address," 02:04–05:20.

Black reminds students that they didn't spend "all this money" not to achieve their dreams, and, employing a *Sankofan* rhetoric reminiscent of the Black preaching tradition, recites a litany of Black progenitors and forebears of history who made it despite all odds. He tells graduates that the faculty are there, not because they don't have anywhere else to teach, but because everyday at CAU they see God—in the beauty, diversity, and purposefulness of their Black students. Black calls names of previous CAU graduates, reminding the class of 2024 that they stand in a lineage and legacy of people who exemplify "Black genius." He then shares an original poem he penned using the tagline "They Not Like Us," a take off the diss track written and recorded by rapper Kendrick Lamar. Black does not diss anyone, but rather reminds graduates that they are set apart to be great. Black concludes his speech with a call to dance that evokes an ancestral ring shout:

> So when people doubt you, graduates, get up and dance. When people laugh at you, graduates, get up and dance. When people don't believe in you, graduates, get up and dance. When people think they've gotten over on you, dance. Ain't no telling what you gon' be. . . . When it looks like all hope is gone, get up and dance, baby, dance!"[2]

Black's address epitomizes the core of Afrofuturism, engaging a *Sankofan* hermeneutic with contemporary realities and futuristic visions, employing arts and technology to craft something unique and original that inspires and galvanizes individual and collective potential. His phrase "Here they come, y'all, here they come!" is both affirmation and advance notice, to any and all who think Black folx will somehow be forgotten or omitted from the world's future that they are mistaken. His recitation of the plethora of professional arenas graduates are poised to enter, as well as his litany of ancestors and graduates, serve as reminders that pressing forward in the face of doubt and despair while accomplishing goals are not new achievements for Black peoples, but part of a legacy of generativity and perseverance long since begun.

---

2. Black, "Commencement Address," 14:35–15:06.

Epilogue

I wrote this book with a similar motivation—to remind Black peoples and the world of our ubiquitous, powerful presence in history and to assert and affirm that we will continue to be present, regardless of whatever machinations may be perpetrated against us. Further, I wrote this book as a testament to the power of Black ancestral music to nurture, sustain, and future us, as it has always done, and to assist the Black church to engage Afrofuturism, both as concept and framework. Across centuries, pastors and preachers of every hue have publicly decried and disparaged Blackness (both racially and ontologically) and the Black church for daring to encourage her citizenry to be politically and socially astute and aware. I am hoping that Black faith communities will embrace Afrofuturism as a cogent, joyful response, reclaiming all that has been transformative for us, including our ancestral music, a spiritual technology and resource beyond parallel.

"Music is the vehicle through which to merge with a larger cosmic consciousness,"[3] and Black peoples have historically found our ways to higher planes/higher ground/higher consciousness through our music. We have never been godless, powerless, or hopeless; we have always had access to alternate dimensions and spheres from which we drew strength, resilience, and fortitude. Although "Blackness" was assigned to us as a racial construct and often used pejoratively, we have always had the power to define and envision ourselves as God's good and beautiful creation. May we allow the spiritual power in our music to propel us forward into a place where our Blackness is no longer the singular defining or determining characteristic of our identity, but just one more beautiful quality we possess in a future we gloriously and unapologetically inhabit.

Here we come, y'all, here we come . . .
Ad astra.

---

3. J. Brown, *Black Utopias*, 9.

Bibliography

Abbington, James, ed. *Readings in African American Church Music and Worship.* 2 vols. Chicago: GIA, 2001, 2014.

Agawu, Kofi. *The African Imagination in Music.* New York: Oxford University Press, 2016.

Allen, Lisa. *A Womanist Theology of Worship: Liturgy, Justice, and Communal Righteousness.* Maryknoll, NY: Orbis, 2021.

Alwood, J. K. "The Unclouded Day." Hymnary, 1885. https://hymnary.org/text/o_they_tell_me_of_a_home_far_beyond_the_.

Anderson, Reynaldo. "Critical Afrofuturism: A Case Study in Visual Rhetoric, Sequential Art, and Postapocalyptic Black Identity." In *The Blacker the Ink: Constructions of Black Identity in Comics and Sequential Art,* edited by Frances Gateward and John Jennings, 171–92. New Brunswick, NJ: Rutgers University Press, 2015.

Asante, Molefi Kete, and Kariamu Welsh Asante. *African Culture: The Rhythms of Unity.* Trenton, NJ: Africa World, 1990.

Association of Religion Data Archives. "Ethiopian Orthodox Church (1959–Present)—Religions Group." ARDA, 2020. https://www.thearda.com/us-religion/group-profiles/groups?D=299.

Barrett, Leonard E. *Soul-Force: African Heritage in Afro-American Religion.* C. Eric Lincoln Series on Black Religion. New York: Anchor, 1974.

Bebey, Francis. *African Music: A People's Art.* Translated by Josephine Bennett. Brooklyn, NY: Lawrence Hill & Co., 1975. Kindle.

Binns, John. *The Orthodox Church of Ethiopia: A History.* Library of Modern Religion. London: Tauris, 2017.

Black, Daniel P. "Commencement Address." YouTube, May 18, 2024. From Clark Atlanta University. https://youtu.be/F25OAzSzhfM?si=A-1SudfLwWGDAX8T.

Blassingame, John W. *The Slave Community: Plantation Life in the Antebellum South.* New York: Oxford University Press, 1972.

Bibliography

Board of Regents of the University System of Georgia. "A Brief History of the Internet." Online Library Learning Center, n.d. https://www.usg.edu/galileo/skills/unit07/internet07_02.phtml.

Boyd, Joe Dan. *Judge Jackson and the Colored Sacred Harp*. Montgomery: Alabama Folklife Association, 2002.

Brooks, Gennifer. "The Creation of an Africana Worship Ritual: Baptism in the Shouters of Trinidad." In *Companion to "The Africana Worship Book*," edited by Valerie Bridgeman Davis and Safiyah Fosua, 62–68. Nashville: Discipleship Resources, 2007.

Brown, Jayna. *Black Utopias: Speculative Life and the Music of Other Worlds*. Durham: Duke University Press, 2021.

Brown, William Wells. "Narrative of William W. Brown: A Fugitive Slave." In *Four Fugitive Slave Narratives*, edited by Robin W. Winks, 40–41. Menlo Park, CA: Addisson-Wesley, 1969.

Cannon, Katie Geneva. *Katie's Canon: Womanism and the Soul of the Black Community*. New York: Continuum, 1995.

Chireau, Yvonne P. *Black Magic: Religion and the African American Conjuring Tradition*. Berkeley: University of California Press, 2003.

Cone, James H. *The Spirituals and the Blues: An Interpretation*. 2nd ed. Maryknoll, NY: Orbis, 1992.

Coptic Orthodox Diocese of the Southern United States. "Coptic Liturgy." SUS Copts, n.d. https://www.suscopts.org/pdf/copticchurch/liturgy1.pdf.

Costen, Melva Wilson. *African American Christian Worship*. 2nd ed. Nashville: Abingdon, 2007.

———. "African Roots of Afro-American Baptismal Practices." In *The Black Christian Worship Experience*, edited by Melva Wilson Costen and Darius Leander Swann, 23–42. Rev. ed. Black Church Scholars 4. Atlanta: ITC, 1992.

———. *In Spirit and in Truth: The Music of African American Worship*. Louisville: Westminster John Knox, 2004.

Cummings, George C. L. "The Slave Narratives as a Source of Black Theological Discourse." In *Cut Loose Your Stammering Tongue: Black Theology in the Slave Narrative*, edited by Dwight N. Hopkins and George C. L. Cummings, 33–46. 2nd ed. Louisville: Westminster John Knox, 2003.

Earls, Aaron. "Four Reasons People Haven't Come Back to Church." Lifeway Research, June 7, 2023. https://research.lifeway.com/2023/06/07/4-reasons-people-havent-come-back-to-church/.

———. "Six Reasons Millennials Aren't at Your Church." Lifeway Research, May 16, 2014. https://research.lifeway.com/2014/05/16/6-reasons-millennials-arent-at-your-church/.

Editor. "Spiritual Technologies: Exploring the Intersections Between Religion and Modern Tech." ReligionLink, Nov. 14, 2022; updated Jan. 23, 2024. https://religionlink.com/source-guides/spiritual-technologies-exploring-the-intersections-between-religion-and-modern-tech/.

Bibliography

Floyd-Thomas, Stacey. "Writing for Our Lives: Womanism as An Epistemological Revolution." In *Deeper Shades of Purple: Womanism in Religion and Society*, edited by Stacey Floyd-Thomas, 1–15. Religion, Race, and Ethnicity. New York: NYU Press, 2006.

Frazier, E. Franklin. *The Negro Church in America*. Sourcebooks in Negro History. New York: Schocken, 1974.

Goff, James R., Jr. *Close Harmony: A History of Southern Gospel*. Chapel Hill: University of North Carolina Press, 2002.

Halvorson-Taylor, Martien. "EGMT 1510, Mythmaking: What Do Myths Do for Us and How Do They Do It?" University of Virginia College of Arts and Sciences, n.d. Course description. https://gened.as.virginia.edu/egmt-1510-mythmaking-what-do-myths-do-us-and-how-do-they-do-it.

Herskovitz, Melville J. *The Myth of the Negro Past*. Boston: Beacon, 1941.

Holmes, Barbara A. *Liberation and the Cosmos: Conversations with the Elders*. Rev. ed. Minneapolis: Fortress, 2023.

Hopkins, Dwight N. *Shoes That Fit Our Feet: Sources for a Constructive Black Theology*. Maryknoll, NY: Orbis, 1993.

Karenga, Maulena. "Black Religion." In *African American Religious Studies: An Interdisciplinary Anthology*, edited by Gayraud S. Wilmore, 271–300. Durham: Duke University Press, 1989.

LaFleur, Ingrid. "Visual Aesthetics of Afrofuturism." YouTube, Sept. 25, 2011. From TEDx Fort Green Salon. https://youtu.be/x7bCaSzk9Zc?si=JmzW8uslKBWVtMW6.

Levine, Lawrence W. *Black Culture and Black Consciousness: Afro-American Folk Thought from Slavery to Freedom*. New York: Oxford University Press, 1977.

Lexicon of Design Research. "Futuring." Lexicon of Design Research, n.d. http://www.lexiconofdesignresearch.com/lexicon/texts/futuring.

Lincoln, C. Eric, and Lawrence H. Mamiya. *The Black Church in the African American Experience*. Durham: Duke University Press, 1996.

Lozano, Teresita D. "'It's a Coptic Thing': Music, Liturgy, and Religious Identify in an American Coptic Community." *World of Music*, n.s., 4 (2015) 37–55. https://www.jstor.org/stable/43774593.

Lucas, David. "20/20 Foresight: Envisioning the Future Workplace." Digital Workplace Group, Sept. 18, 2024; updated Apr. 17, 2025. https://digitalworkplacegroup.com/20-20-foresight-envisioning-the-future-workplace/.

Magis Center. "The Purpose of a Myth: Insights from J. R. R. Tolkien and Mircea Eliade." Magis Center, Mar. 24, 2023. https://www.magiscenter.com/blog/purpose-of-myths.

Martin, Clarice J. "Womanist Biblical Interpretation." In *Dictionary of Biblical Interpretation*, edited by John H. Hayes, 657–58. Nashville: Abingdon, 1999.

Maultsby, Portia K. "The Use and Performance of Hymnody, Spirituals, and Gospels in the Black Church." In *Readings in African American Church Music and Worship*, edited by James Abbington, 1:77–98. Chicago: GIA, 2001.

Bibliography

Mbiti, John S. *African Religions and Philosophy*. 2nd ed. Portsmouth, NH: Heinemann, 1990.

Meinardus, Otto F. A. *Two Thousand Years of Coptic Christianity*. Cairo: American University in Cairo Press, 1999.

McKinnis, Leonard Cornell, II. *The Black Coptic Church: Race and Imagination in a New Religion*. Religion, Race, and Ethnicity. New York: NYU Press, 2023.

Nierenberg, George, dir. *Say Amen, Somebody*. St. Louis: GTN, 1982. DVD.

Nketia, J. H. Kwabena. *The Music of Africa*. New York: Norton, 1974.

Oatman, Perry. *Ethiopian Orthodox Tewahedo Church: A Beginner's Guide; Journey Through Tradition and Belief*. N.p.: Self-published, 2024.

Oomen, Jeroen, et al. "Techniques of Futuring: On How Imagined Futures Become Socially Performative." *European Journal of Social Theory* 25 (2022) 252–70. https://journals.sagepub.com/doi/10.1177/13684310209888826.

Paris, Peter J. *The Spirituality of African Peoples: The Search for a Common Moral Discourse*. Minneapolis: Fortress, 1995.

Peoples, Dottie. *He's an On-Time God*. Atlanta: AIR, 1994. Compact disc.

Raboteau, Albert J. *Canaan Land: A Religious History of African Americans*. Religion in American Life. New York: Oxford University Press, 2001. Kindle.

———. *Slave Religion: The "Invisible Institution" in the Antebellum South*. Rev. ed. New York: Oxford University Press, 2004.

Ray, Robert. *He Never Failed Me Yet*. Milwaukee: Jenson, 1982.

Really Good Innovation. "Futuring." Really Good Innovation, n.d. https://www.reallygoodinnovation.com/glossaries/futuring.

Richards, Dona Marimba. *Let the Circle Be Unbroken: The Implications of African Spirituality in the Diaspora*. Trenton, NJ: Red Sea, 1989.

Robertson, Marian, et al. "Music, Coptic." *Claremont Coptic Encyclopedia*, n.d. CE:1715a–1747b. https://ccdl.claremont.edu/digital/collection/cce/id/1446/rec/1.

Rucker, Walter. "Conjure, Magic, and Power: The Influence of Afro-Atlantic Religious Practices on Slave Resistance and Rebellion." *Journal of Black Studies* 32 (2001) 84–103. https://doi.org/10.1177/002193470103200105.

Sanders, Cheryl J. "In the World, but Not of It." In *Readings in African American Church Music and Worship*, edited by James Abbington, 1:99–114. Chicago: GIA, 2001.

Sellassie, Sergew Hable, and Belaynesh Mikael. "Worship in the Ethiopian Orthodox Church." Ethiopian Orthodox Tewahedo Church Faith and Order, Dec. 1970. From *The Church of Ethiopa: A Panorama of History and Spiritual Life* (Addis Ababa: EOTC). https://www.ethiopianorthodox.org/english/ethiopian/worship.html.

Smith, Gregory A., et al. "In U.S., Decline of Christianity Continues at Rapid Pace." Pew Research Center, Oct. 17, 2019. https://www.pewresearch.org/religion/2019/10/17/in-u-s-decline-of-christianity-continues-at-rapid-pace/.

Bibliography

Smith, Theophus H. *Conjuring Culture: Biblical Formations of Black America*. Religion in America. New York: Oxford University Press, 1994.

Sneed, Roger A. *The Dreamer and the Dream: Afrofuturism and Black Religious Thought*. New Suns: Race, Gender, and Sexuality in the Speculative. Columbus: Ohio State University Press, 2021.

Sobel, Mechal. *Trabelin' On: The Slave Journey to an Afro-Baptist Faith*. Princeton, NJ: Princeton University Press, 1988.

Southern, Eileen. *The Music of Black Americans*. 3rd ed. New York: Norton, 1997.

Spencer, Jon Michael. "The Rhythms of Black Folks." In *"Ain't Gonna Lay My 'Ligion Down": African American Religion in the South*, edited by Alonzo Johnson and Paul Jersild, 39–51. Northwestern Series in Transnational. Columbia: University of South Carolina Press, 1996.

Spiritual Technologies Project. "About Spiritual Technologies Project." Spiritual Technologies Project, n.d. https://www.spiritualtechnologiesproject.org/what-we-do.

Stewart, Carlyle Fielding, III. *Black Spirituality & Black Consciousness: Soul Force, Culture and Freedom in the African-American Experience*. Trenton, NJ: Africa World, 1999.

Summers, Myrna, and the Refreshing Springs COGIC Choir. *Uncloudy Day*. By J. K. Alwood. Newark: Savoy, 1981. Album.

Taryor, Nya Kwiawon. *Impact of the African Tradition on African Christianity*. Chicago: Strugglers' Community, 1984.

Waters, Donald J., ed. *Strange Ways and Sweet Dreams: Afro-American Folklore from the Hampton Institute*. Boston: Hall & Co., 1983.

Whalum, Wendell P. "Black Hymnody." In *Readings in African American Church Music and Worship*, edited by James Abbington, 1:167–84. Chicago: GIA, 2001.

Williams, Delores S. *Sisters in the Wilderness: The Challenge of Womanist God-Talk*. Maryknoll, NY: Orbis, 1993.

Wilmore, Gayraud S. *Black Religion and Black Radicalism: An Interpretation of the Religious History of Afro-American People*. 3rd ed. Maryknoll, NY: Orbis, 1998.

Wilson-Dickson, Andrew. *The Story of Christian Music: From Gregorian Chant to Black Gospel; An Authoritative Illustrated Guide to All the Major Traditions of Music in Worship*. Minneapolis: Fortress, 2003.

Womack, Ytasha L. *Afrofuturism: The World of Black Sci-Fi and Fantasy Culture*. Chicago: Hill, 2013.

———. "I Came to Africa on a Spaceship." In *Afrofuturism: A History of Black Futures*, edited by Kevin M. Strait and Kinshasha Holman Conwill, 48–56. Washington, DC: Smithsonian, 2024.

Work, John W. "The Negro Spiritual." In *Readings in African American Church Music and Worship*, edited by James Abbington, 1:15–26. Chicago: GIA, 2001.

Index

Page numbers followed by *fig* refer to a figure on that page. Page numbers followed by "n" and another number refer to a footnote on that page.

a cappella singing, 18–19, 23
abolitionism, 100–101
Aedesius, brother of Saint
    Frumentius, 19–20
aerophones, 6–7, 119
affirmation, 99
African American churches
    after emancipation, 47–50,
        100–101, 102
    Black Coptic Church (BCC),
        25–26, 27
    charismatic worship in, 127–28
    children and young people in,
        xiii–xiv, 26–28, 52–53, 69,
        70
    decline and pushback against
        specific genres in, 34–35,
        50–53, 59, 81–82
    declining attendance in, 85–92
    Eurocentric theologies in, 102,
        121–22
    from Great Migration, 25–26,
        56–57, 119
    importance of preserving
        historic genres in, 35–40,
        62–66, 67–69, 72–75,
        112–20
    liturgies in, 51–52, 111–12
    music genres across the year in,
        75–76, 77*fig*–79*fig*, 79–81
    political activism in, xiv, 100–
        101, 128
    teaching about historic genres
        in, xv, 68–72, 80–81
    See also invisible institution
        (brush/hush arbor worship)
African and African American
    ancestral music
    in African traditional religions,
        1–14
    in Afrofuturism, 112–20
    gospel music, 54–66
    hymnody, 41–53
    in Orthodox Churches, 15–28
    spirituals, 29–40
    See also African traditional
        religions and music;
        Afrofuturism; gospel music;
        hymnody; spirituals
African Benevolent Society, 45

Index

African Methodist Episcopal Church, 100
African Methodist Episcopal Zion (AMEZ) Church, 48, 100
African traditional religions and music, 1–14
   African American churches' rejection of, 102, 120–22
   High God in, 12, 33, 97, 101, 104–5, 107–8
   influence on African American sacred music, 31, 35–39, 43, 49, 116–17
   instrumental music in, 3–8
   key beliefs in, 13–14, 104–9
   rites and rituals in, 2, 6, 7, 9–12, 96–98, 121, 125–28
   role of music in, 2–3
   time as conceived in, 129
   vocal music in, 8–9, 13
   worship music in, 13–14
Africans, enslaved
   African traditional religions and, 9–12, 96–98, 107–9, 125–28, 129
   anti-Black messaging towards, 26, 37, 64, 96, 101–2
   hush harbor worship of, 11–12, 22–23, 64, 97–100, 109, 116–17, 129
   in Second Great Awakening, 44
   in slaveholders' churches, 37, 42, 98, 101–2, 116–17
   spirituals of, 29–40 (*see also* spirituals)
   uprisings by, 99, 128
AfricansinAmerica term, xvin4
Afrofuturism, 83–133
   African and Black cosmologies and theologies in, 104–11, 120–22
   background on, xv–xvi, 93–98
   "Conjure" practice in, 124–28
   in countering anti-Blackness, 94, 95–96, 101–2, 114–15, 120–30, 132–33
   "futuring" concept in, 83–85, 93
   historic music genres in, 112–20
   historical worship themes in, 98–101
   implications of declining church attendance for, 85–92
   liturgies in, 111–12
   mythmaking in, 122–24
   Orthodox Churches and, 23–28
   time-space exploration in, 128–30
"Ain't Got Time to Die" (spiritual), 39–40, 74
"Ain't-A That Good News" (spiritual), 36
air and wind instruments, 6–7, 119
"Alabaster Box" (gospel song), 78*fig*
alghaita (musical instrument), 7
"All God's Chillun Got Shoes" (spiritual), 32, 38–39
"All the Way My Savior Leads Me" (hymn), 46
Allen, Richard, 47–48
Allen, William, 31
Alwood, J. K., xi
Anaphora (liturgy), 18, 20, 21
ancestors, veneration of, 97, 105
Anderson, Douglas L., Sr., xiv
Anderson, Reynaldo, xvi, 96
Andraé Crouch Singers, 60
Anglicans, 42, 45, 102
Anglo-descended cultures, music in, 3, 8, 41–43, 45
   See also white Christians
Anianus of Alexandria, 16
antebellum period. *See* Africans, enslaved
anthems, 66
anti-Blackness

Index

countering of, 26, 94, 95–96, 101–2, 114–15, 120–30, 132–33
of white Christians, 37, 64, 101–2, 120–22
Apostolic churches, 47, 100
Ark of the Covenant, 19
arranged compositions. *See* hymnals and arranged compositions
Asante, Kariamu, 10–11
Asante, Molefi, 10–11
"Ase" affirmation, 121
Ash Wednesday, 77*fig*
"At the Cross" (hymn), 49
Athanasius of Alexandria, 20
Azusa Street Revival, 47, 57

Baker, Anita, 61
Bantu traditional music, 4
Baptists, 44–45, 47, 48, 56n4, 100
Barrett, Leonard, 3, 105, 106
Barrett Sisters, 63
basalt stones, 8
Basil, Saint, 17
Bebey, Francis, 3, 5, 8n10
"Because He Lives" (hymn), 49
"Before This Time Another Year" (hymn), 117
begena (musical instrument), 22
Best, George, 121
biblical interpretation, 95, 110, 123–24
biblical narratives, 64–65, 120, 123–24, 128
Biggie Smalls, 61
Binns, John, 19, 20
Black, Daniel P. "Omotosho," xvin4, 131–32
Black Coptic Church (BCC), 25–26, 27
"Black" label, xvin4
Black peoples. *See* African American churches; African and African American ancestral music; African traditional religions and music; Africans, enslaved; Afrofuturism
"Blessed Assurance" (hymn), 46, 49
Bliss, Phillip, 47
blues, 29, 58, 59, 66
Bodin, Jean, 121
body percussion, 22, 23, 118
Bouknight, Lillian, 77*fig*
bow-lute, 6
Bradbury, William, 47, 53
Bremer, Fredrika, 55
Brewster, W. Herbert, 78*fig*
Brooks, Gennifer, 10
Brown, Brenton Gifford, 78*fig*
Brown, Jayna, 128–29
Brunson, Milton, 60
brush arbor worship. *See* invisible institution (brush/hush arbor worship)
Buckley, Horace L., Sr., xiv
"Buked and Scorned" (spiritual), 40, 79*fig*
Busta Rhymes, 61
Butler, Octavia, xv

Caesar, Shirley, 58, 79*fig*
call-and-response, 35, 36, 43, 76, 116, 119
"Calvary" (spiritual), 37–38
Calvinist theology, 102
camp meetings, 43–45, 54–55
Campbell, Lecresia, 77*fig*
Cane Ridge Camp Meeting, 44
Cannon, Katie Geneva, 29–30, 31–32, 109–10, 123
cantillation classes, 24–25
capitalism, 130
The Caravans, 58, 63, 79*fig*
Carr, Kurt, 78*fig*
catechism classes, 42, 98
"Certainly, Lord" (spiritual), 76

Index

"Change Me, O God" (gospel song), 77*fig*
chant. *See* vocal music
"A Charge to Keep I Have" (hymn), 49, 116–17
charismatic worship, 127–28
children, xiii–xiv, 24–25, 26–28, 52–53, 69, 70
"Children, We All Shall Be Free" (spiritual), 39
Chireau, Yvonne, 125, 126–27
Chisholm, Thomas, 78*fig*
choral and ensemble singing
    in gospel music, 58–59, 60, 62, 66, 119
    in Orthodox Churches, 19, 23
    praise choruses, 51, 52, 53
    preservation of historic genres in, xv, 34–35, 67–68, 70, 74
chordophones (stringed instruments), 6, 22, 23, 60, 66
choruses (part of song), 46, 55–56, 63, 65, 66
chronos time, 128
church attendance, 51–52, 85–92
church musicians, xiv, 21, 50, 52–53, 74, 75, 82
    See also choral and ensemble singing
Church of England, 42
Church of God in Christ (COGIC), 48, 57, 100
Church of the Holy Virgin, 16
churches. *See* African American churches; Orthodox Churches; worship services
"The Church's One Foundation" (hymn), 49
"City Called Heaven" (spiritual), 36, 77*fig*, 83
Clara Ward Singers, 58
Clark Atlanta University, xvin4, 131–32

Clark Sisters, Dr. Mattie Moss Clark and the, 58, 60
Clay, Thomas, 77*fig*
Cleveland, James, 58, 60, 61, 77*fig*, 118
Coleridge-Taylor, Samuel, 31
Coley, Daryl, 78*fig*
Colored (Christian) Methodist Episcopal (CME) Church, 47, 48, 100
Colored Union Church, 45
"Come Thou Fount of Every Blessing" (hymn), 73
Commissioned (gospel choir), 60
communal worship and spirituality
    in African traditional religions, 11, 13, 38–39, 98, 100, 105–6
    in Afrofuturism, 111–12
    in children's upbringing, xiii–xiv, 25
    contemporary churches' lack of, 86, 87–88, 90–91
    in Coptic Orthodox Church, 25
    in gospel music, 63, 65
    hymnody in, 50, 116
    individualistic view of salvation vs., 122
Communion (Eucharist), 18, 20, 21
compassion, 105
Cone, James, 29, 30, 33
Congregationalists, 42
"Conjure" practice, 124–28
contemporary gospel music, 60–62, 76n2, 77*fig*–79*fig*, 81
convention songs, 46
Coptic Orthodox Church, 16–19, 19n7, 23–25
    See also Black Coptic Church (BCC)
cosmology, African. *See* African traditional religions and music
Costen, Melva, 9, 10, 17, 42–43, 101, 105

Index

COVID-19 pandemic, 89
creativity, 94–95
creeds, 13, 18
Crosby, Fanny, 46, 77*fig*
Crouch, Andraé, 60
Cummings, George, 109
curriculum, music education, 71–72, 80–81
cymbals, 18
Cyril, Saint, 17

dabtaras (Ethiopian Orthodox musicians), 21
Daily Offices, 20
dances, 5, 8, 22, 23, 55, 132
  See also ring shout
deacons, 18–19, 21
death, 10, 33–34, 37, 108, 129
"Deep River" (spiritual), 32, 40, 75
deities. *See* God and gods
deliverance services, 128
Dery, Mark, 93
design and innovation research, 84
Dett, R. Nathaniel, 31
"Didn't My Lord Deliver Daniel" (spiritual), 33, 37, 64
digital footprint, 86, 88–89
Dillard, Ricky, 78*fig*
diversity, 87, 95
Divine Liturgy, 17–19, 20–22, 23–25
"Done Made My Vow to the Lord" (spiritual), 36
Dorsey, Thomas A., 58–59, 78*fig*
"Dr. Watts's hymns" style of singing, 43
drums, 3–6, 21–22, 23, 66, 119
Du Bois, W. E. B., 30, 97

Earls, Aaron, 85–89
education, music. *See* music education
Egypt and Egyptian Christianity, 15, 16–19, 19n7, 23–25
  See also Black Coptic Church (BCC)
embellishment, 8n10, 36
emotional expression
  Black Methodists' avoidance of, 48
  in enslaved Africans' worship, 99–100
  in gospel music, 118–19
  in Holiness-Pentecostal churches, 56, 57
  in Second Great Awakening, 44
  in spirituals, 30, 32, 36, 39–40, 114
ensemble singing. *See* choral and ensemble singing
enslaved Africans. *See* Africans, enslaved
entertainment, music for, 2
eschatology, 34, 36, 129
ethics, 34, 109–11
Ethiopian Christianity, 17, 19–22, 23
  See also Black Coptic Church (BCC)
Eucharist, 18, 20, 21
European cultures, music in, 3, 8, 41–43, 45
  See also white Christians
European Journal of Social Theory, 84
evangelicalism, 122
evangelism, 14, 16, 19–20, 42–44
Evening Offering of Incense, 17, 18–19
"Everlasting God" (gospel song), 77*fig*
"Every Time I Feel the Spirit" (spiritual), 38, 73–74
evil, 34, 108
Ezana of Aksum, King, 19
"Ezekiel Saw de Wheel" (spiritual), 34

Facts and Trends (website), 85

Index

"Father, I Stretch My Hands to Thee" (hymn), 49, 116–17
Festival of American Folklife, 46
fiddles, 22
First Great Awakening, 42–43, 122
Fisher, Miles Mark, 31
Fisk Jubilee Singers, 31n7
Floyd-Thomas, Stacey, 110
flutes, 7
folklore, 29, 30, 31–32, 98, 106–7, 123
    See also storytelling
"Follow the Drinking Gourd" (spiritual), 32
"For Every Mountain" (gospel song), 78*fig*
Franklin, Ernest, 79*fig*
Franklin, Kirk, 61
Frazier, E. Franklin, 59
freedom. *See* liberation and freedom
friction drum, 5
Frumentius, Saint, 19–20
"futuring" concept, 83–85, 93

Gardner, Newport, 45
Ge'ez language, 17, 20
generational gaps, 51–52, 85–89
"getting religion," 99, 109
GIA Publications, 48
"Give Me a Clean Heart" (gospel song), 77*fig*
"Give Me Jesus" (spiritual), 33–34
"Glory, Glory, Hallelujah (Since I Laid My Burdens Down)" (spiritual), 40
"Go Down, Moses" (spiritual), 33, 37, 64, 74
"Go 'Way, Satan, I Doan Mind You" (spiritual), 34
God and gods
    in African traditional religions, 10, 13, 33, 37, 96–97, 101, 104–5, 106, 107–8, 116–17, 125
    in gospel music, 61, 62, 63, 65, 74–75, 119–20
    in hymnody, 73, 116–17
    in *kairos* time, 128
    mythmaking and, 122
    in spirituals, 33, 34, 37–38, 64
"God Is" (gospel song), 74
Goff, James, 44, 55–56
gospel music, 54–66
    contemporary gospel music, 60–62, 76n2, 77*fig*–79*fig*
    hymnody and, 46, 48, 51, 52, 53, 54–56, 118
    meaning making from, 62–66
    origins of, 54–59
    preservation of historic, 74–75, 77*fig*–79*fig*, 118–20
Gospel Music Workshop of America, 58
Great Awakenings, 42–45, 54–56, 122
"Great Day" (spiritual), 74
"Great Is Thy Faithfulness" (hymn), 50, 78*fig*
Great Migration, 25, 56–57
Gregory, Saint, 17
griots (professional musicians), 3, 6
guest musicians, 71, 79–80, 81
"Guide Me, O Thou Great Jehovah" (hymn), 78*fig*, 116–17
"Guide My Feet" (spiritual), 74
guitars, 60, 66
Guy (band), 61

Hall, Aaron, 61
Hall, Derrick, 78*fig*
"Hallelujah, Salvation, and Glory" (gospel song), 74
Hammond organ, 66, 119
hand piano, 7, 8
harps, 6
Hawkins Family, 60, 61
"He Got Up" (spiritual), 34

Index

"He Never Failed Me Yet" (gospel song), 64, 65
"He Never Said a Mumblin' Word" (spiritual), 33–34, 79*fig*
healing rituals, 6, 125–26, 127
herders, 7
"Here's One" (spiritual), 40
Herskovitz, Melville, 33
"He's an On-Time God" (gospel song), 64, 65
"He's Got the Whole World in His Hands" (spiritual), 39, 74
High God, 12, 33, 97, 101, 104–5, 107–8
"Higher Ground" (hymn), 78*fig*
Holiness-Pentecostal churches, 47, 56–57, 57n7, 100
Holmes, Barbara, 103
"Holy, Holy, Holy" (hymn), 49, 73
Holy Qurbana (Divine Liturgy), 17–19, 20–22, 23–25
Holy Spirit
  in African American sacred music, 38, 41, 114, 117
  African traditional religions and, 67, 98, 108–9
  "Conjure" practice and, 127–28
  in *kairos* time, 130
hope, 33, 34, 36, 38, 99
Hopkins, Dwight, 105, 106–7
horns, 7
"Hosanna, Loud Hosannas" (hymn), 79*fig*
Houghton, Israel, 79*fig*
hour-glass drum, 4
Houston, Whitney, 61
"How Excellent" (gospel song), 74–75
"How I Got Over" (gospel song), 74
hush harbor worship. *See* invisible institution (brush/hush arbor worship)
hymn lining, 43, 115–17
hymnals and arranged compositions
  for African American denominations, 47–48, 117, 118
  gospel music in, 58, 118
  for Holiness-Pentecostal congregations, 57
  in music education, 45, 53, 73
  of spirituals, 31, 36
hymnody, 41–53
  contemporary decline and pushback against, 50–53, 81
  history of, 41–50
  preservation of, 73, 77*fig*–79*fig*, 115–18

"I Am Thine, O Lord" (hymn), 46, 77*fig*
"I Believe I'll Go Back Home" (spiritual), 34, 78*fig*
"I Done Died" (hymn), 116
"I Find No Fault in God" (gospel song), 79*fig*
"I Got Shoes" (spiritual), 64
"I Know I Am a Child of God" (hymn), 41, 117
"I Love the Lord, He Heard Me Cry" (hymn), 49, 116–17
"I Shall Not Be Moved" (spiritual), 40
"I Sing the Mighty Power of God" (hymn), 49
"I Want Jesus to Walk with Me" (spiritual), 37–38, 77*fig*
"I Want To Be Ready" (spiritual), 131
"I Will Bless Thee, O Lord" (gospel song), 118
"I Will Call Upon the Lord" (gospel song), 74–75
identification-ascertainment hermeneutic, 110
idiophones, 7–8, 18, 22

Index

"If I Perish (I'm Going to See the King)" (gospel song), 64
"If You See My Savior" (gospel song), 58, 63
"I'll Overcome Someday" (gospel song), 58
"I'll Tell It Wherever I Go" (gospel song), 63
"I'm Going to Live the Life I Sing About" (gospel song), 58
"I'm Gonna Sing When the Spirit Says Sing" (spiritual), 74
"I'm Just a Poor Wayfaring Stranger" (spiritual), 36
"I'm So Glad Trouble Don't Last Always" (spiritual), 34
"I'm Troubled in Mind" (spiritual), 40
imagination, 94–95
improvisation, 36, 47, 66, 119
"In That Great Getting Up Morning/Ride On, King Jesus" (gospel song), 79*fig*
innovation and design research, 84
instruments, 3–8, 21–22, 52–53, 66, 118, 119
See also a cappella singing
Internet, 86, 88–89
invisible institution (brush/hush arbor worship)
    African traditional religions and, 11–12, 97–98, 109
    as counter to slaveholders' churches, 64
    music of, 22–23, 116–17, 129
    worship themes in, 98–100
"It Is Well with My Soul" (hymn), 47
"It's a Highway to Heaven" (gospel song), 58
"I've Been 'Buked and I've Been Scorned" (spiritual), 40, 79*fig*
"I've Got Peace Like a River" (spiritual), 38

Jackson, Judge, 45–46
Jackson, Mahalia, 58, 63, 78*fig*
Jesus, 33–34, 37–38, 61, 62, 108, 120, 122
"Jesus, Blessed Savior" (gospel song), 74–75
"Jesus Is a Rock in a Weary Land" (gospel song), 77*fig*
"Jesus Loves Me, This I Know" (hymn), 47
"Jesus Walked This Lonesome Valley" (spiritual), 77*fig*
"Jesus Will Work It Out" (gospel song), 64
Johnson, James Weldon, 31
Johnson, John Rosamond, 31
Jones, Absalom, 47
Jones, Charles Price, 57
joy, 99
"Joyful, Joyful, We Adore Thee" (hymn), 73
Judaism, 19
judgment and justice, 34, 36, 37, 38, 95, 108
"Just as I Am" (hymn), 47
"Just for Me" (gospel song), 79*fig*

kairos time, 128, 130
kalimba (musical instrument), 7, 8
Kebra Nagast (Ethiopian Christian narrative), 19
Kee, John P., 61
"King Jesus Is A-Listenin'" (spiritual), 78*fig*
"King of Kings" (spiritual), 33
kinship, 105–6
konde (musical instrument), 6
Krehbiel, Henry F., 31

LaFleur, Ingrid, 94
Lamar, Kendrick, 132
Lawrence, Donald, 78*fig*
leadership roles, 88

Index

Lent, 76, 77fig–79fig
Leonard, Tasha Cobbs, 78fig
Leslie-Rule, Michaela, 112
"Let It Rise" (gospel song), 74–75
Levine, Lawrence, 39
Lexicon of Design Research, 84
liberation and freedom
    in African traditional religions, 37, 107–8
    in Afrofuturism, 95, 103, 109–12, 123–24, 131–33
    in "Conjure" practice, 126, 127, 128
    in gospel music, 61–62, 64–65
    in hymnody, 116
    in spirituals, 32, 33, 34, 36, 37–38
    time-space exploration in, 129
    in worship, 92, 98–99
"Lily of the Valley" (spiritual), 33
lined/metered hymns, 43, 73, 115–17
"Listen to the Lambs" (spiritual), 33–34
lithophones, 8
"Little David, Play on Your Harp" (spiritual), 75–76
"Little Innocent Lamb" (spiritual), 33, 78fig
liturgical seasons, 76, 77fig–79fig
liturgies, 17–19, 20–22, 23–25, 51–52, 91, 92, 111–12
    See also worship services
Lobo, Jerome, 21–22, 23
"Lord, I Want to Be a Christian" (hymn), 77fig
"Lord, Who Throughout These Forty Days" (hymn), 77fig
"Lord, You Are Good" (gospel song), 79fig
"The Lord Is My Light and My Salvation" (gospel song), 77fig
"Lord Keep Me Day by Day" (gospel song), 74

"The Lord Will Make a Way Somehow" (gospel song), 58
"The Lord Will Make a Way Somehow" (hymn), 50
"Love Divine, All Loves Excelling" (hymn), 73
"Love Lifted Me" (hymn), 47
Lozano, Teresita, 23–25
lutes, 6
lyres, 22

Mann, Tamela, 77fig
Mark, the Evangelist, Saint, 16, 17
Marsh, J. B. T., 31
Martin, Roberta, 58, 63
Martin, Sallie, 58, 63
"Mary, Don't You Weep" (spiritual), 15, 34, 37, 64, 65
"Mary's Little Boy-Child" (spiritual), 33
masenqo (musical instrument), 22
Mason, Charles Harrison, 57
"Master Blaster" (reggae song), 60
Maultsby, Portia, 47
"May the Work I've Done Speak for Me" (gospel song), 63
Mbiti, John, 3, 10, 33, 101, 104, 106, 125
McClurkin, Donnie, 79fig
McGrath, Hugh, 46
McKinnis, Leonard, 25–26, 27
meaning, 62–66, 90–92
medicine men, 6
Meinardus, Otto, 16
melisma, 18, 22–23
melody, 31, 36, 43, 73, 75–76
Menelek I, Emperor of Ethiopia, 19
metered/lined hymns, 43, 73, 115–17
Methodist Episcopal Church, 57, 100
Methodist Episcopal Church South, 45
Methodists, 44–45, 47, 48, 56n4, 57

Index

milliennials and generational gaps, 51–52, 85–89
mirliton (musical instrument), 7
missionaries and evangelism, 14, 16, 19–20, 42–44
Monastery of the Holy Virgin, 16
Montesquieu, Charles de Secondat, baron de, 121
Moody, Dwight Lyman, 46
moral work, 2
Morning Offering of Incense, 17, 18–19
Moses, 33, 37, 64, 65, 74
"Move On Up a Little Higher" (gospel song), 63, 78*fig*
Murphy, William, 77*fig*
music. *See* African and African American ancestral music
music education
    in catechism classes, 42
    on historic genres, xv, 68–72, 80–81
    in Orthodox Churches, 21, 24–25
    piano lessons in, xii, 52–53
    shape-note system in, 45
musical instruments, 3–8, 21–22, 52–53, 66, 118, 119
    See also a cappella singing
mvet (musical instrument), 6
"My Good Lord's Done Been Here" (spiritual), 34
mythmaking, 122–24
    See also folklore; storytelling

National Baptist Convention of America, 100
National Baptist Convention, USA, 48, 100
National Convention of Choirs and Choruses, 58
nature, 106
"Near the Cross" (hymn), 46

Nebuchadnezzar II, King of Babylonia, 65
Negro spirituals. *See* spirituals
"Never Would Have Made It" (gospel song), 62
New Jersey Mass Choir, 60, 118
"Nobody Knows the Trouble I've Seen" (spiritual), 39–40
Norwood, Dorothy, 58
"Not Like Us" (diss track), 132

"O God, Our Help in Ages Past" (hymn), 49
Oatman, Johnson, Jr., 78*fig*
oboes, 7
Offering of Incense, 17, 18–19
"Oh, Freedom" (spiritual), 32, 39–40
"Oh, How I Love Jesus" (hymn), 50
"Oh, Mary, Don't You Weep" (spiritual), 15, 34, 37, 64, 65
"Oh Lord, How Come Me Here?" (spiritual), 32, 36
"The Old Ark's A-Moverin" (spiritual), 38
"One Nation Under a Groove" (funk rock song), 61
O'Neal Twins, 63
"On-Time God" (gospel song), 64, 65
Ordo Communis (liturgy), 20
organ, 66, 119
Orthodox Churches, 15–28
    in Afrofuturist projections, 23–28
    Coptic Orthodox Church, 16–19, 19n7, 23–25
    Ethiopian Orthodox Church, 19–22, 23
    music of enslaved Africans and, 22–23

Palm Sunday, 79*fig*
Parham, Charles, 57n7

INDEX

Paris, Peter, 104
Parliament Funkadelic, 61
"Pass Me Not, O Gentle Savior" (hymn), 46
Patterson, Cicero, 26
"Peace, Be Still" (gospel song), 74, 118
"Peace in the Valley" (gospel song), 58
Pentecostal churches, 47, 56–57, 100
percussion
    in African traditional music, 3–6, 7–8
    in gospel music, 66, 119
    in hymnody, 52–53, 118
    in Orthodox Churches, 18, 21–22, 23
"Perfect Praise" (gospel song), 74–75
Pew Research Center, 85, 89
piano lessons, xii, 52–53
political activism, xiv, 100–101, 128
praise choruses, 51, 52, 53
"Praise Him" (gospel song), 74–75, 118
prayers, 17, 18, 20
"Precious Lord" (gospel song), 58, 74
Presbyterians, 42, 44–45
priests, 18, 20, 21, 24, 25
professional musicians, 2, 3, 6, 21
    See also church musicians
proverbs, 67, 106–7
psalm singing, 41–42, 43
published collections and arrangements. See hymnals and arranged compositions
Puritan theology, 102

al-Qusiya, 16

Raboteau, Albert, 30, 44, 108
racism. See anti-Blackness
Ragin, Ron, 112
Ray, Robert, 65
reading, of music, 45, 53, 73
Reagon, Bernice Johnson, 29n2
Really Good Innovation, 84
Reformed churches, 42
refrains, 48, 55, 63, 66
ReligionLink (website), 113
research, 68–69, 82, 84–85, 111
resistance, 95, 98–99, 126, 127, 128
    See also liberation and freedom
resurrection, 34, 37, 108
"Revelation 19:1" (gospel song), 74
revival movements, 42–45, 47, 54–56, 57, 122
rhythm, 3–4, 5, 18, 36
Richards, Dona Marimba, 10, 11
"Ride On, King Jesus" (spiritual), 36, 79*fig*
"Ride On, King Jesus/In That Great Getting Up Morning" (gospel song), 79*fig*
Riley, Teddy, 61
ring shout, 5, 11, 23, 132
rites and rituals, 2, 6, 7, 9–12, 96–98, 121, 125–28
    See also liturgies
Roberts, T. Carlis, 112
Robey, Don, 78*fig*
Rodney, Winston, 118
Rowe, James, 47
Rushen, Patrice, 61

"Safe from Harm" (gospel song), 79*fig*
"Safety" (gospel song), 77*fig*
Salt-N-Pepa, 61
salvation, 122
Sanctified churches, 47, 56–57, 100
Sanders, Cheryl, 56
Sankey, Ira, 46–47
Sankofan lens, 27, 115, 124, 132
Sanza (musical instrument), 7, 8
Sapp, Marvin, 62
"Savior, Like a Shepherd Lead Us" (hymn), 73
Scarface, 61
science fiction (sci-fi), xi–xii

Index

"Search Me, Lord" (gospel song), 78*fig*
seasons, 8, 76, 77*fig*–79*fig*
Second Great Awakening, 43–45, 54–56, 122
"Seek the Lord" (spiritual), 78*fig*
Seymour, William, 57n7
shape-note system, 45
Sheba, Queen of, 19
"Shut de Do" (spiritual), 34
"silk-stocking" churches, 56
sin, 34
singing. *See* vocal music
singing schools, 45
single-headed drum, 5
"Sinner, Please Don't Let This Harvest Pass" (spiritual), 34
sistrums, 22
Sjostran, Janice, 78*fig*
slavery. *See* Africans, enslaved
slit drum, 4
Smallwood, Richard, 118
Smith, Theophus, 9
Smith, Willie Mae Ford, 54, 58, 61–62, 63
Smithsonian Institution, 46
Sneed, Roger, xv, xvi
Sobel, Mechal, 3–4
social media, 86, 88–89
Society for the Propagation of the Gospel in Foreign Parts, 42
sociology, 84, 85, 93
"The Solid Rock" (hymn), 47
Solomon, King of Israel, 19
"Sometimes I Feel Like a Motherless Child" (spiritual), 32, 36
songbooks. *See* hymnals and arranged compositions
"Soon One Morning" (spiritual), 34
sorrow songs, 30
Southern, Eileen, 41
Southern Presbyterians, 45
Spence, Peter, 48

Spencer, Jon Michael, 4, 5–6
spirit possession, 109
"spiritual but not religious" people, 86, 87
spiritual songs, 55–56
Spiritual Technologies Project (STP), 112–13
spiritual technology, 112–20
spirituals, 29–40
 background on, 29–31
 in choirs, 34–35, 66, 74
 contemporary pushback against, 35, 81–82
 as folklore, 29, 30, 31–32, 123
 gospel music and, 64–65
 relevance and preservation of, 34–40, 73–74, 75–76, 77*fig*–79*fig*, 114–15
 as theological and ethical statements of belief, 33–34, 37–39
St. Mark Coptic Orthodox Church (Englewood), 24–25
"Standing in the Need of Prayer" (spiritual), 34
"Steal Away" (spiritual), 32
Stewart, Carlyle Fielding, III, 11–12
"Stomp (Remix)" (gospel song), 61
storytelling, 3, 6, 122–24
 See also folklore
stringed instruments, 6, 22, 23, 60, 66
suffering, 33–34, 37–38, 108
Sunday School Publishing Board, 48
"Sunshine in My Soul" (spiritual), 74
survival, 98
"Sweet Little Jesus Boy" (spiritual), 37–38

Take 6 (gospel sextet), 61
Taryor, Nya, 9
teaching, of music. *See* music education

Index

technology, xii, xiii, 60–61, 66, 86, 88–89, 119
   See also spiritual technology
testimonies, 62–63
Tharpe, Rosetta, 61
Third Great Awakening, 45
Thompson, Linda, 79*fig*
Thompson Community Choir, 60
Threlfall, Jeanette, 79*fig*
thumb piano, 7, 8
time-space exploration, 128–30
Tindley, Charles Albert, 53, 57–58
"'Tis So Sweet to Trust in Jesus" (hymn), 47
"To God Be the Glory, Great Things He Has Done" (hymn), 73
Tolkien, J. R. R., 123
"Total Praise" (gospel song), 118
traditional gospel music. *See* gospel music
triangle (musical instrument), 18
Tri-City Singers, 78*fig*
Trinity, 13, 108–9
Trinity Church, 42
"Trouble in My Way" (gospel song), 78*fig*
trumpets, 7
trust, 86–87
tsenatsil (musical instrument), 22
Tucker, Ira, Jr., 78*fig*

Ubuntu, 106
"The Unclouded Day" (hymn), xi
United Methodist Church, 48
University of Virginia, 123

visions, 99, 109
vocal music
   in African traditional music, 8–9, 13
   gospel music, 54–66
   hymnody, 41–53
   in Orthodox Churches, 18–19, 21, 22, 23, 24–25

spirituals, 29–40
   See also gospel music; hymnody; spirituals

"Wade in the Water" (spiritual), 37, 64, 73–74
Walker, Albertina, 58, 78*fig*
Walter Hawkins Love Alive Choir, 60
Ward, Clara, 58, 63
Watanabe, Esther, 118
water drum, 5
Waters, Donald, 127
Watts, Isaac, 42, 47
websites, 86, 88–89
Weheliye, Alexander, xv–xvi
Wesley, Charles, 47
Western cultures, music in, 3, 8, 41–43, 45
   See also white Christians
Whalum, Wendell, 49
"What a Friend We Have in Jesus" (hymn), 49, 73
"What a Mighty God We Serve" (gospel song), 74–75
"What Wondrous Love Is This" (hymn), 79*fig*
"When I Die, I Want to Die Easy" (spiritual), 33–34
"When Sunday Comes" (gospel song), 78*fig*
White, Benjamin Franklin, 45
white Christians
   African American churches' imitation of, 48, 102
   anti-Blackness of, 37, 64, 101–2, 120–22
   catechism classes of, 42, 98
   in Great Awakenings, 42–45, 55, 122
   in Holiness-Pentecostal churches, 57
   hymnody of, 41–43, 116–17
   salvation theology of, 122
Williams, Delores, 110

Index

Williams, Dewey, 46
Williams, Oscar, 77*fig*
Williams, William, 78*fig*
Wilson-Dickson, Andrew, 19–20
Winans, Benjamin (BeBe), 61, 79*fig*
Winans, Priscilla (CeCe), 61, 78*fig*
Winans family, 61
wind and air instruments, 6–7, 119
Wiregrass Singers, 45
Withers, Bill, 61
Womack, Ytasha, xv–xvi, 93, 94, 115
wombi (musical instrument), 6
women and womanism, 29–30, 58, 59, 109–11
Wonder, Stevie, 60
"Wonderful Words of Life" (hymn), 47
"Woo-Hah!! Got You All in Check" (hip hop song), 61
work music, 2
World Future Society, 84
worship services
    in African traditional religions, 13–14
    Afrofuturist lens for, 85–93, 94–95, 97–102, 111–12, 121–22, 127–28, 130
    decline and pushback against specific genres in, 34–35, 50–53, 59, 81–82
    declining attendance in, 85–92
    of early African American churches, 47–50, 56–57, 100, 102, 119
    of enslaved Africans, 11–12, 22–23, 64, 97–100, 109, 116–17, 129
    importance of preserving historic genres in, 35–40, 62–66, 67–69, 72–75, 112–20
    music genres across the year in, 75–76, 77*fig*–79*fig*, 79–81
    in Orthodox Churches, 17–19, 20–22, 23–25
    teaching of historic genres for, 68–72, 80–81
    of white Christians, 41–45, 48, 55, 57, 116–17

xylophone, 8

Yacob, Father (priest), 24, 25
Yared, Saint, 21
"Yes, God Is Real" (hymn), 50
Yoruba people, 4, 121n24
"You Brought the Sunshine" (gospel song), 60
"You Know My Name" (gospel song), 78*fig*
young people, xiii–xiv, 24–25, 26–28, 52–53, 69, 70, 85–89
"You're the Lifter of My Head" (gospel song), 78*fig*

zithers, 6
Zulu traditional music, 1
Zurara, Gomes Eanes de, 121

www.ingramcontent.com/pod-product-compliance
Lightning Source LLC
Chambersburg PA
CBHW030857170426
43193CB00009BA/640